WINNING THROUGH PARTICIPATION

Meeting the Challenge of Corporate Change
With the *Technology of Participation*

The Group Facilitation Methods
of the Institute of Cultural Affairs

D0556199

Laura J. Spencer
for The Institute of Cultural Affairs

Foreword by Rosabeth Moss Kanter
Author of *When Giants Learn to Dance* and *The Change Masters*

KENDALL/HUNT PUBLISHING COMPANY
4050 Westmark Drive   Dubuque, Iowa 52002

CREDITS

Shashkin, Marshall. *A Manager's Guide to Participative Management* and *ParticipativeManagement Remains An Ethical Imperative.* Reprinted by permission of publisher, from AMA Periodicals Review, Spring 1986, Copyright © 1986 and from AMA Management Briefing 1982, Copyright © 1982. American Management Association, New York. All rights reserved.

Naisbitt, John and Patricia Aburdene. *Reinventing the Corporation.* New York: Warner Books. Copyright © 1985 Megatrends, Inc. Reprinted by permission.

W. P. Anthony, *Participative Management.* Copyright © 1978 Addison-Wesley Publishing Co., Inc., Reading, Massachusetts. From pages 9–11 and 4–15. Reprinted with permission.

Toffler, Alvin, *Future Shock.* New York: Bantam. 1970. Reprinted with permission.

Hayes, Robert H., *Why Strategic Planning Goes Awry,* April 20, 1986. Copyright © 1986 by The New York Times Company. Reprinted with permission.

Prokesch, Steven, *Remaking the American C.E.O.,* January 25, 1987. Copyright © 1987 by The New York Times Company. Reprinted by permission.

Excerpts from *American Spirit: Visions of a New Corporate Culture* by Lawrence M. Miller, Copyright © 1984 by Lawrence M. Miller. Used by permission of William Morrow and Co., Inc.

Leadership Development from IMAGE, April 1987, pp. 2–5. ICA, Bombay, India.

Foreword by Rosabeth Moss Kanter, author of *When Giants Learn to Dance* and *The Change Masters.*

Research and writing assistance: Steve Sanders
Editors: Don Smith and Jeanette Almada
Graphics: Lynette Ladysmith
Photographs on pages 73–74 and 161: Don Cherry.

Dedicated to the people of Fifth City, whose spirit shaped the *Technology of Participation*.

ACKNOWLEDGMENTS

This book, and indeed, the development of the *Technology of Participation* would not have been possible without the countless organizations around the world who, over the past thirty-five years, participated in developing, refining and custom-designing applications of *ToP*.

The ICA extends its thanks to the hundreds of ICA staff and colleagues who contributed their ideas, stories and time in researching data, interviewing clients for case studies and checking the manuscript for accuracy at various stages of its development.

We wish to extend our gratitude to Dr. Marty Seldman, who provided the inspiration, the enthusiasm and the practical leadership that launched this effort.

Special thanks to the Chicago office of the ICA for providing the personnel, the resources and the environment that got this project off the ground and those whose support brought it to completion.

CONTENTS

Song, Story and Symbol Workshop
Action Planning Workshop

PART FOUR: Benefits of the *Technology of Participation*

FOREWORD

By Rosabeth Moss Kanter

Author of *When Giants Learn to Dance* and *The Change Masters*

In today's fast-paced world of constant change and pressure for responsiveness, all organizations must dance to new rhythms. And so the Giants are finally waking up and learning to dance.

The Giants are those machine-like bureaucracies—large corporations or government agencies—that have become sluggish, slow moving, and unresponsive. Now they are trying to be like dancers, more agile, flexible, and innovative, faster on their feet in planning and able to execute their plans with greater effectiveness. One of the most important dance steps they are learning is to involve their people in problem-solving and planning.

Companies like Motorola and Ford—two of the more remarkable corporate transformations of recent years—attribute much of their success in changing from sleeping Giant to agile competitor to their participative management and employee involvement programs. These programs mobilize and motivate the workforce to contribute their best ideas through problem-solving teams. Ford's results, in particular, have led the company to proclaim that "Quality is Job #1"—and indeed, the quality ratings of Ford cars began to lead the pack a few years ago, and Ford outperformed General Motors in profits in 1987 on a much smaller revenue base.

Public sector as well as private sector organizations are enjoying the fruits of well-managed, carefully-structured participation programs, as they wake up to the realities of a world of rapid change. The Governor of Minnesota and the Chairman of Control Data Corporation, for example, co-chair the Steering Committee for STEP ("Strive Toward Excellence in Performance"), a pioneering effort to improve state government through employee-initiated project teams using participative methods. Dozens of teams have been chartered to improve productivity and service quality through creative innovations and partnerships between agencies. Among the creative solutions: a joint effort between the public works department and the bureau of prisons to place ex-prisoners in good jobs.

Across the management landscape, in Europe as well as the United States, participation is an idea whose time has come. I remember that the term "participation" had radical connotations in the late 1960s, smacking of the demands of student leaders and community organizers for more involvement in the rule-making of the institutions governing them. But by the late 1980s, a growing body of evidence of the success of bottom-line-oriented businesses using participative processes—as found in my book, *The Change Masters* and transmitted in my consulting work—has given the idea respectability. Now the major question for the 1990s is not WHETHER to use participation but HOW.

Why are so many diverse kinds of organizations embracing participative management principles? What do organizations gain from the use of participative planning and problem-solving? I see five benefits, beginning with the most concrete and immediate, but also including some that are longer-term enhancers of productivity and effectiveness.

• *The specific plans themselves—strategies, solutions, action plans.* A world of rapid change requires constant planning and replanning, as circumstances change, as new competitors burst on the scene, as events require mid-course correction. So organizations need more planning and problem-solving today; they cannot run on automatic pilot. Thus, bringing together those with expertise and a stake in an issue is the fastest way to tackle problems, address opportunities, and define new directions.

• *Greater commitment—and ability—to implement decisions and strategies.* When people participate in a planning process, they are certainly more likely to be committed to the plans, because they have talked them through, because the plans reflect their own thinking, and because the group has developed consensus. This is just common sense— although it did take scores of careful social science studies to convince some managers of this obvious truth. But organizations also find their people *better equipped* to carry out the plans when they participate in shaping them because they are more knowledgeable and informed. They better understand the needs, the goals, and where their own responsibilities fit in with those of others.

• *More innovation—a larger portfolio of ideas.* Involvement of more people in the planning process, especially a mixture of people with different perspectives, generates new insights into problems and encourages a fresh look at opportunities. The cross-fertilization from a group bringing diverse backgrounds to a planning task can sometimes result in breakthrough strategies. I call this ''Kaleidoscope thinking''—the ability to challenge traditional assumptions and define new patterns and possibilities.

• *A common framework for decision-making, communication, planning, and problem-solving.* The team-building effects of participation extend well beyond the ''high'' of a successful planning session. A group with a common vocabulary and methodology for working together—e.g., a sense of how to conduct a meeting—does not have to argue over procedure but can go right to work. Thus, meetings become more productive, and teamwork is enhanced.

• *Encouragement of initiative and responsibility.* This is the least tangible and longest-term benefit, and perhaps the most important. People who have been involved in participative planning are more likely to feel a sense of ownership for their part of the organization. They are more likely to take action when they see a problem or an opportunity, rather than assume it's someone else's responsibility.

But it is not enough to see the *benefits* of participative planning and problem-solving; it is important to develop a methodology for managing the process, as ICA has done in its Technology of Participation. After all, group sessions can sometimes degenerate into chaos. Teams can take longer to decide anything than individuals. And as I have seen from working with numerous companies at their executive retreats, unguided ''participation'' can all-too-often result in frustration as nothing significant seems to be accomplished or—the opposite—as enthusiastic groups generate dozens and dozens of exciting action items, too many to be acted on effectively.

So, in order to make participation work, it is essential to have a good structure. Clear limits and guidelines and leadership are important in making an empowering, freedom-generating process like participation work. People can slide into neurotic behavior when given freedoms they cannot handle. True ''freedom'' is not the absence of structure—letting the employees go off and do whatever they want—but rather a clear structure which enables people to work within established boundaries in an autonomous and creative way. It is important to establish for people, from the beginning, the ground rules and boundary conditions under which they are working. Without structure, groups often flounder un-productively, and the members then conclude they are merely wasting their time. The fewer the constraints given a team, the more time will be spent defining its structure rather than carrying out its task.

Total freedom, with no limits set, will not occur in a business organization anyway. But the limits can be vague, unclear, contradictory, hidden and subject to guesswork. So the group might make a large number of false starts before it finally learns what is permis-sible and what is not. It might spend most of its time discussing *how* to decide rather than deciding. Too many choices, too much up for grabs can be frustrating. Anchors are neces-sary, something to bounce off of, some constraints or criteria or goals.

Thus, turning over a task or an issue to a group of organization members with no guidelines, objectives, constraints, or limits can be extremely ineffective; yet some people (both advocates and detractors) think that this is what participation must mean. Respon-sible parties (managers or leaders) do not give up all their control or responsibility for results just because they are involving a wider circle of people; nor ought they to leave the participating members to flounder without help. It is significant in this respect that par-ticipation works better where the parties involved in it are strong, and there is clear leader-ship in the organization. I have seen, for example, in union-management committees that these do not work where either the union or management is weak. The benefits of par-ticipation do not seem to occur in stalemate situations where no one has enough power to generate action. In short, *leadership*—the existence of people with power to mobilize and guide others, to see that the results of planning sessions are used—is an important in-gredient in making participation work. It is almost a paradox: Participation requires better leadership than a machine-like bureaucracy. The leadership tasks may be shared or rotated, but they must be performed. And one of the leadership roles is to provide a structure for participative planning.

But structure means workable, empowering ground rules, like those in the Technology of Participation. Structure does not imply the imposition of mindless formulas for action, such as rote motions specified in minute detail that substitute for thinking. This is the problem with many packaged programs that have been sold to U.S. companies under the "participation-and-" label: participation and strategic planning or quality improvement or culture change. Too many American companies use the "appliance model of organization change," as my colleague Barry Stein called it: buy a complete program, like a "quality-circle package," from a dealer, plug it in , and hope that it runs by itself. Thus, the opposite extreme from no-structure is *over*structuring participative activities with no thought to the appropriateness of the model for the place where it is being used, and with the elimination of one of the values of participation to employees: the chance to be more creative, exert more influence over work decisions. A balance must be struck. For the Giants to dance, they need both discipline and the freedom to innovate.

Of course, a good participative process is not enough by itself. The successful implementation of participative planning is directly tied to the culture of the organization and the work area. Critical factors conducive to successful participation include:

• Fostering good communication, a necessity to make the process work. This means both the formal communication process through meetings, memos, and other paperwork, as well as the informal processes—gathering across areas to form networks, to exchange ideas, to share insights about events in different parts of the organization.

• Encouraging people to set high performance goals and to aim to reach them through continuous improvement and innovation. People should see value in improving the level of quality or productivity in their area, for both themselves and the organization. They should be willing to set goals to do this, seeing change as an opportunity rather than a threat.

• Giving people the self-esteem and tools to take initiative to solve problems. People should be "empowered" to take action, otherwise they will be reluctant to get involved. They need the tools—the expertise and knowledge, resources, and management support—as well as the inner confidence to take on and resolve problems.

• Rewarding and recognizing contributions. One of my favorite Change Masters at one of the best dancing Giants of the corporate world puts this principle succinctly: Make everyone a hero. If more people are to get involved in planning the organization's work, they need to get credit for it. The above-and-beyond hard work of solving problems and leading change should be applauded, praised and publicized.

The Institute of Cultural Affairs should also be applauded, praised and publicized for its decades of teaching Giants to dance. In this useful book are a series of lessons and techniques applicable to organizations of all sizes and types as they learn to use participation to meet the challenge of change.

INTRODUCTION

What sets the winners apart from the also-rans and losers in today's tough, competitive international business arena?

Specific isolating factors have distinguished successful companies. Acknowledged authorities have noted a loosening of the often rigid, authoritarian style that characterized most businesses and organizations as the most significant change within winning organizations in recent times. Winners in today's demanding marketplace are characterized by a management style that stresses:

- flexibility and responsiveness to change,
- innovative thinking,
- informal communication,
- continuing education and learning,
- visionary leadership and emphasis on quality.

But there's another factor, one that links all of these values together into what most experts see as the management style of the future. It's called **"participation"**, or "participative management."

Management consultant Ralph Barra, for example, suggests that "companies that will survive are going to be participative." Industrial and organizational psychologist Marshall Sashkin reports that "clear research evidence shows that participative management improves performance." Thousands of companies have responded to such heraldings. Giants such as 3M have implemented participative programs as the vital matrix for building winning teams.

But few, if any, of these respected books, studies and dissertations tell how to transform participative management from theory into reality. This book is designed to bridge that gap. It explains why participation works and why a participative approach is so critical to getting the best results in today's—and tomorrow's—management environment.

Furthermore, this book tells exactly how participation can be put to work in the factory, at the sales counter and throughout the business office. Through a system called the *Technology of Participation*, this book explains vital and underlying principles and examines step-by-step techniques that have yielded winning performances for leading companies.

Developed by the Institute of Cultural Affairs (ICA), the *Technology of Participation (ToP)* has achieved outstanding results just about everywhere it's been tried. From the aisles of neighborhood stores to the boardrooms of Fortune 500 companies *ToP* has boosted progress, improved performance and yielded impressive management results. The

McDonald's Corporation, for example, increased sales 10-20% in markets where managers and franchise owners applied *ToP* methods. Houston's Hughes Tool Company introduced a manufacturing process that yielded a productivity index of over 110%. A subsidiary of the Sun Chemical Company of New York increased its sales by 40% in just six months using *ToP* methods. One of Japan's Nichii Department Stores raised its sales rating from 37th all the way up to 15th within a year of implementing *ToP* techniques.

Those are just a sampling of the success stories reported by companies that have profitably applied *ToP* methods. Equally important, those companies gained long-term benefits beyond the realization of short-term profit goals.

Participation—getting employees involved in the company's planning and problem-solving tasks—can animate and inspire a project team, a department, even an entire corporation. When employees are actively brought into the mainstream by working together as a team to develop a plan for improving company operations, for example, they become highly motivated to carry it out. This surge of commitment can ignite the energy, enthusiasm, and creativity essential to a company's success in today's rugged competitive environment.

For over 35 years the ICA has worked with individuals, communities and organizations to develop methods to maximize creativity and corporate action. During its early years the ICA worked largely with local communities, helping them to plan and implement comprehensive social and economic development. Because of the voluntary and informal nature of these groups, techniques were needed that generated and sustained motivation and commitment. Under these circumstances there were no bosses, no employees and no monetary incentives to spur productivity. There was only commitment from those involved to their communities and to their plans for revitalization. Tasks were complex. They included developing plans and implementing programs to boost local business development, education, health care systems, agricultural development, sanitation, housing, and more. Achieving these tasks involved mobilizing and training task forces of volunteers to help develop and implement various plans. Massive research was required to locate available resources and services. Sophisticated interface with business and government was required.

The ICA used it's *ToP* methods for its own internal planning and operations. The methods continued to evolve as ICA staff became adept at modifying and expanding the techniques for virtually all planning and problem-solving tasks. As the ICA expanded to 34 nations, its methods proved effective among groups representing diverse socio-economic and cultural backgrounds. In fact, many deeply divided groups experienced reconciliation as these sophisticated methods enabled them to focus on common visions of the future rather than fractionalized differences.

The ICA's work with local communities led to its becoming the organizing co-sponsor of the International Exposition of Rural Development (IERD). This three-year event researched and brought together practitioners of local development from 54 nations to share and document approaches that work in local community development.

As businesses and government organizations became aware of the group planning and leadership development skills so effectively executed by the ICA among local communities, they sought ICA facilitators for their own planning or problem-solving sessions. In response to such varied corporate and organizational requests, several programs were developed under numerous names and for various purposes. *LENS* (Leadership Effectiveness and New Strategies) and *Strategic Planning and Implementation* are two of the most widely-known of these programs. Many customized applications were also developed in response to specific situations and requests. Corporate response to such programs has been enthusiastic. High praises have been common among corporate clients for *ToP's* ability to:

- produce action plans that get done;
- accomplish in a short time, usually 2 days, what would have taken weeks or even months to accomplish with traditional planning methods;
- bring together a wide range of perspectives, resulting in a comprehensive plan;
- generate commitment on the part of participants that resulted in quick, effective implementation;
- build team spirit; and
- follow-up with strategic reviews that kept plans on track, even when circumstances changed.

Many organizations around the world have used these methods extensively to bring about alignment within large complex organizations, or to affect major change within internal structures and/or operating strategies. Several of these organizations have trained their own staff in *ToP* methods and use them daily. As you read through the chapters of this book, you will hear about many of these organizations and see how they put these methods to work.

The ICA's clients have included Amoco, Bell Labs, Coca Cola, Colgate Palmolive, Conoco, DuPont, General Mills, Honeywell, IBM, Kellogg, McDonald's, 3M, Mobil, Procter & Gamble, Sears, Shell, Time Life and United Airlines, to name just a few. Above all, the tough-minded managers of those major companies want solid, measurable results from any investment they make. *The Technology of Participation* has demonstrated over and over again that it can deliver those results.

However, the ICA's client base extends far beyond this blue-chip group of companies. As a number of case histories in this book will show, *ToP* methods have helped all types and all sizes of organizations throughout the world, be they commercial or not-for-profit, public or private, local in scope and service or world-class.

From basic manufacturing companies to those tapping, harnessing and selling natural resources, from hospitals to high tech industries, from restaurant chains to religious groups, from chambers of commerce to neighborhood development groups, from schools to department stores, and from insurance companies to computer firms, organizations are solving problems and gaining an edge on the competition by putting *ToP* methods to work.

As a bank manager recently participating in one of the ICA's programs noted, "There is absolutely no organization that could not benefit from your program."

Many organizations have discovered that the more *ToP* methods are used, the more useful they become. Many clients who engage *ToP* initially for problem solving or strategic planning find that it works equally well for team building, leadership development, redefining the corporate mission and philosophy, and strengthening organizational development. Indeed, this book is written partially in response to the encouragement from clients to stop hiding our light under the proverbial bushel and partially in response to our own recognition that participative management is a key to future success and that corporate awareness of that fact is growing. The term *Technology of Participation (ToP)* is new, a handle by which to refer to a variety of methods that have been packaged into numerous programs and called many different names. The methods are not new. They have been developed, tested and refined over thirty-five years, proving successful with organizations of all types, of all sizes, of all industries and in all parts of the world.

This book is designed to guide the reader through the three basic *ToP* methods and describes how to apply these methods to achieve results in many tasks.

Part One sets the stage, describing the emergence of participative management in response to the changing economic environment. If you are already a believer in participation and are looking for practical help in applying it, you may wish to skip these first two chapters. If you are yet to be convinced, or are trying to convince someone else of the values of participation for today's organizations, these chapters offer forceful insight.

Part Two explains both the theory and the practice of the fundamental *ToP* methods. These methods are building blocks to more complex applications, but they also stand alone and can be put to use in hundreds of situations every day. With practice, they become a way of life.

Part Three describes some of the many customized *ToP* applications. Based on programs developed for and successfully used with clients, these chapters illustrate the kaleidoscope of opportunities available to those who master the *Technology of Participation*.

Participative management, and particularly the *Technology of Participation,* represents a management style whose time has arrived—for many reasons but especially for one: it offers managers tools and techniques needed to harness and master the sometimes harrowing winds of change now sweeping through their companies, their markets, their communities and the world at large.

PART ONE

A New Generation of Participation

CHAPTER 1

Changing Times Call for Changing Management

If there is anything that today's management experts agree upon, almost without reservation, it is that our time is one of rapid change. Consider these thoughts by leading thinkers about management in these times:

Change is the only constant we all face.

James D. Robinson
Chairman
American Express Company

The ability to adapt to a constantly changing world is not only a requisite for success, but for survival.

Stephen B. Hardis
Vice Chairman
Eaton Corporation

The modern business world is anything but static. . . . Advances in technology are causing products and companies to change more rapidly than ever before. Business strategies that look promising one day look obsolete the next.

Regis McKenna
The Regis Touch

The businesses that survive on the corporate battlefield, like the species that survive in nature, are those which can adapt, developing new strategies as conditions warrant.

Paul Solman and Thomas Friedman
Life and Death on the Corporate Battlefield

We have a choice. We can either be victims of change or we can be co-creators of our organization's future. The future is paved with complexity and ambiguity, but to travel it is both the challenge and the adventure we face.

Leroy Fahle
Health Care Executive

It is likely you can recall as many similar comments about change and its effects from your own recent conversations. But a critical question remains. How can we learn to adopt the creative and enthusiastic response of Leroy Fahle's "co-creators of the future," rather than being mere victims, overwhelmed by change? This book will address that question by describing a management approach that has proven effective in responding to change—as Tom Peters would say, "thrives on chaos."

First, however, let's examine some of the faces of change.

The Changing Marketplace—Competition is the Watchword

Competition is the watchword in today's business community. Even schools, hospitals and government agencies (such as the United States Postal Service) are forced to compete as corporations do, for survival. While competition is not new, its scope and intensity in today's organizations is very new. Perhaps this newly intense and broadened competitive style brings the most significant contributions to the massive changes sweeping today's business world.

What has brought about this shift? Recession and stagflation in the U.S. economy in the mid-70's slowed the world's real economic growth to less than 1 percent in 1974. Consumer confidence dropped. In the late 70's and early 80's, inflation and soaring interest rates resulted in a contracting world economy, a fluctuating dollar on world currency markets and rising foreign competition in one industry after another.

"The biggest change," says J.E. Newall, president of DuPont Canada, "has been that we've moved permanently into an era of **low growth**. When our markets were growing rapidly, we, along with our competition, all grew. The best just grew faster. Now to grow we have to steal it from the competition, and that is a lot tougher challenge."

One outstanding feature of the competitive environment in which we live is that it is **truly global**. National economies are bitter contenders on the global economic battlefield. Manufacturing takes place in developing nations where labor is cheap. Mergers and acquisitions that provide access to new resources and new markets are commonplace.

Another outstanding feature of today's competitive environment is the **rapid rate of technological development**. The rise of the information age is transforming the thinking, organization and action of the business world and of society as a whole.

In fact, many trends in business today can be seen as direct responses to the intense competition companies face. Most of them result in a **restructuring of the organization** in one form or another.

Downsizing, or "trimming the fat" has become mandatory in today's slow-growth economy. Organizations must demand exceptional productivity from every employee. There is no margin in corporate budgets for "extra baggage." In most organizations the "fat" lies within the ranks of the middle management and these managers are caught in the squeeze. They can anticipate an increased workload or a termination notice.

Divestitures are a form of downsizing at another level. Getting rid of money-losing products or marginal divisions can save a company from depressed stock prices and corporate raiders. This trend, of course, has led to the merger and acquisition fever of the past few years.

Mania over *mergers and acquisitions* has developed in response to corporate races to access new resources and markets, opening up a new era of global sales and manufacturing. Grady Means, international economic director at Coopers and Lybrands, reports that "In the past, international sales for most U.S. companies have ranged from between 10 and 20 percent of the total sales level. Five years from now that will probably go up to 40 percent." Alonzo L. McDonald, former vice-chairman of Bendix Corporation, has attached a name to the newest trend in global manufacturing. In his *Harvard Business Review* article in November of 1986, McDonald referred to this trend as the "floating factory." Instead of one giant factory owned by a single corporation, McDonald asserts that companies are shifting to networks of smaller plants, owned by clusters of companies. Each plant makes a few product components and then ships them for assembly at plants near the markets where they will be sold. "A series of small modules located in different places, each contributing flexible portions of a constantly changing, transportable whole" is how McDonald described the concept.

Competition for the greatest market share leads to competition in developing the best product and offering the best customer service. This competition has led to **emphasis on "excellence,"** a notion promoted by Tom Peters and Robert Waterman in their book *In Search of Excellence* and now espoused by corporate leaders seeking the competitive edge. Excellence in product design and production as well as quality in customer service are aided by the ever-developing technology of the information age. We will soon reach an age, says McKenna, when "diversity costs no more than uniformity," due to computer ability to customize products to buyer specifications. The very term "customer service" no longer refers to a complaints department, but to a whole new industry of technical support, repairs and customer training.

Organizations in search of excellence **compete for the best personnel** by offering superior working environments. In order to attract and hold high quality employees, companies are investing more in their employees and their working environment. This includes providing flexible hours, comfortable working conditions, comprehensive benefits and job retraining in skills more suitable to the modern workplace.

All in the name of competition.

The Changing Workforce —People Are the Competitive Edge

"In an industrial society," say John Naisbitt and Patricia Aburdene in *Reinventing the Corporation,* "the strategic resource is capital. In the new information society, that key resource has shifted to information, knowledge, creativity. And there is only one place where the corporation can mine this valuable new resource—in its employees."

Naisbitt and Aburdene go on to say that "today's workforce is younger, better educated and increasingly female."

The workforce is **younger** and **better educated** because of the influx of "baby boomers" who reached maturity in the early 70's, swelling the workforce by 30% over the past 12 years. Naisbitt and Aburdene predict that by 1990 baby boomers will constitute 54% of all U. S. workers. This baby boom generation has the highest average level of education in U.S. history.

There are many reasons for the **influx of women** into the workforce. The economy, the women's revolution, higher levels of education for women and lower birth rates are just a few. Naisbitt and Aburdene sum up the trend by saying: "We are moving to a time when virtually all women will work at paying jobs." After all, they note, "Today as many women in their twenties and thirties work as men in their twenties and thirties."

Besides demographic differences, today's workforce holds **a new set of values** which are quite different from those of previous generations. The Protestant Work Ethic has been replaced by the notion that work should be fun, or at least personally satisfying. A 1983 Public Agenda Foundation study clearly showed that such values of the new generation are permeating the entire workforce. The top ten factors named by respondents notably evaded previous employment objectives such as higher salaries, job security, or benefits! Rather, the respondents listed:

1. working with people who treat them respectfully,
2. doing work that is interesting,
3. getting recognition for good work,
4. being able to improve their present skills and learn new ones,
5. working for people who listen to their ideas,
6. getting to do some thinking for themselves instead of just following orders,
7. seeing the results of their work,
8. having efficient supervisors,
9. occupying a job that is not too easy, and
10. being kept informed about what is going on in the company.

Just as the changing marketplace requires organizations to change to survive, so does the changing workforce require similar adjustments. To be competitive, companies must be able to attract and keep the best employees. To do this, managers are learning to listen to the demands of their employees.

As mentioned earlier, one demand is that organizations accommodate the lifestyle of the workers. This can mean providing on-site child care for workers with young children, flex-time or job-sharing positions or an on-site health club.

Workers also want to be treated with respect. Rather than mere order-takers, most valuable employees consider themselves to be as intelligent as their superiors and they want that intelligence to be recognized. Workers today value challenge, perhaps more than security. They are bored with work that is too easy. They seek to have their limits continually tested and expanded. Preference for challenge and stimulation is found in the current emphasis on entrepreneurship and "intrapreneurship."

Finally, workers want to participate in corporate decision-making. They are most motivated when they have a say in what they will do and how they will do it. Participation in decision-making offers employees valued opportunities to align personal goals with those of their companies' and enhances the meaningful nature of their work.

The Changing Workplace—Creating the Environment for Change

To maintain the competitive edge corporations must respond to the changes taking place in the marketplace and the workforce. This response is transforming the face, or rather the "guts" of today's corporations. While each organization responds in its own way, there are some common features to the response of those companies that have successfully met the challenge of change.

First, successful companies have **informal** or **lateral lines of communication**, rather than vertical, hierarchical channels. This means workers have the information they need not merely to do their job well, but to be creative in their work. It implies an inherent trust in employees' integrity and intelligence.

Teamwork is another common feature of responsive organizations. Rather than the traditional assembly line or departmental structure of organization, teams are responsible for a task or project from beginning to end. These teams have within them all the skills and resources needed for completion of the task. Each member of the team becomes more aware of the overall task, is therefore more flexible, and ultimately has a greater sense of responsibility. In addition, employees gain the satisfaction of seeing a job completed.

Investing in employees is a key tactic in getting and keeping the best. This includes comprehensive benefits packages, but also involves training or retraining to keep employees' skills up to date with company needs. Companies increasingly find that training can be more economical than laying off old workers and hiring new ones whose salaries must compensate for previously attained training. Training also fosters employee commitment to the company.

An even more effective way of generating employee loyalty and commitment is to give them a **sense of ownership** in the organization. Such loyalty can be accomplished through increasingly popular Employee Stock Ownership Plans (ESOPs), or just as effectively through employee participation in planning and decision-making. Such involvement encourages employee loyalty, sponsoring a genuine belief that their future and that of the organization are linked. Commitment is also boosted by such plans as employee ability to actually influence the future of their organization is enhanced.

All of these factors—the competitive marketplace, the demands of the workforce and the changing workplace—are bringing about a transformation in management style. But this, like the other changes, has not come about overnight.

The Changing Management Style: Responding to Societal Change

The Rise and Fall of Autocracy

In his book, *Participative Management,* William P. Anthony describes the evolution of management styles over the past few centuries. He begins in the time before the Industrial Revolution, prior to the existence of factories or corporations. In that mostly rural world, people lived and worked on farms or were artisans and craftsmen who worked for themselves. Fathers or grandfathers managed family farms, while priests and lords managed the church and the state by decree or tradition. The closest thing to a formal management theory was Machiavelli's *The Prince.* The manager was an **autocrat**. "The role of the manager under this approach is to think and decide," wrote Anthony. "The role of subordinates is to do as they are told and not to ask any questions."

As the Industrial Revolution swept through England and America, the autocratic style of authority was carried over into the factories by managers. Although the chain of command became more complex as bureaucracies developed, it was still vertical, with an autocrat making decisions and those at the bottom of the chain carrying them out.

"This system is premised on the unspoken assumption that the dirty, sweaty men down below cannot make sound decisions," Alvin Toffler observed in *Future Shock.* "Only those higher in the hierarchy are to be trusted with judgment and discretion. Officials at the top make the decisions; men at the bottom carry them out. One group represents the brains of the organization; the other, the hands."

One result of the autocratic style of management was loss of a sense of power over one's own life. "For the first time in history," says industrial and organizational psychologist Marshall Sashkin, "masses of workers lost control not only over what they were to do but how they were to do it." Supervisors assigned tasks, scheduled hours and set wages. Workers felt powerless.

As the Industrial Age matured, however, so did management style. Studies reported how to make workers more productive and admonished managers "not only to hire the workers' hands," Anthony says, "but also . . . their hearts." The prevailing style of management shifted from the autocrat to the **benevolent autocrat.** Though workers still have no power under this system, Anthony says, "managers do try to maintain good relations with subordinates and are concerned with treating subordinates fairly."

Toward the close of the Industrial Revolution the benevolent autocrat was replaced by the **consultor.** Managers began to tap workers' minds as well as their hands and hearts. "The consultive approach to management still vests a lot of authority and power in the managers, but there is one important difference," Anthony comments. "Under this approach, managers do seek input from subordinates. However, they may not use this input. Often they simply bounce their ideas off their subordinates to see their reactions and then they shut the door and make the decision."

This phase in the evolution of management was described by William H. Whyte's book, *The Organization Man,* published in 1956. Whyte portrayed the organization man as a rising middle class manager who not only works for the organization; he belongs to it. In return for a lifetime of financial security and a sense of belonging, Whyte said, such men joined a system that inhibits individual initiative and imagination and the courage to exercise it against group opinion.

The future sketched by Whyte and such authors as Kafka and Orwell in the first half of the twentieth century looked even bleaker. People would increasingly become insignificant cogs in huge organizational machines, frozen into narrow niches and compelled to conform. Bureaucracy would force them into pitiable anonymity, where they would exist as little more than identification numbers, spineless and faceless.

Fortunately, says Toffler, those predictions are very unlikely to come true. Such organizations "are precisely those least likely to dominate tomorrow," he notes. "For we are witnessing not the triumph, but the breakdown of bureaucracy." Naisbitt and Aburdene agree. "Corporations that cling to the outdated philosophy and structure of the old industrial era," they predict, "will become extinct in the new information society."

Competitive Pressures for a New Style

Why are researchers so certain that management style is undergoing radical transformation? It hasn't only been due to the groundswell of protest against regimentation and the growing emphasis on individual rights. More important are the intense global competitiveness and accelerating rate of technology of the Postindustrial Age. Those demands of the changing marketplace, coupled with the pressure for meaning and challenge exerted by the changing workforce, are combining to break autocracy apart.

To begin with, rapid changes in the market and in the speed of production require faster decisions than are possible under the old vertical hierarchies. Toffler reports that today time savings "are feverishly sought by managers fighting to keep up with change. Shortcuts that by-pass the hierarchy are increasingly employed in thousands of factories, offices, laboratories, even in the military. The cumulative result of such small changes is a massive shift from vertical to lateral communication systems. The intended result is speedier communication. This leveling process, however, represents a major blow to the once-sacred bureaucratic hierarchy, and it punches a jagged hole in the 'brain and hand' analogy. For as the vertical chain of command is increasingly by-passed, we find 'hands' beginning to make decisions, too."

Postindustrial technology has also become so complex that it's impossible for managers to have all the answers. The problem, Toffler adds, "is intensified by the arrival on the scene of hordes of experts—specialists in vital fields so narrow that often the men on top have difficulty understanding them. Increasingly, managers have to rely on the judgment of these experts. . . . With no time for decisions to wind their leisurely way up and down the hierarchy, 'advisors' stop merely advising and begin to make decisions themselves."

Moreover, today "companies don't have the time, personnel, or resources to monitor people carefully," say Naisbitt and Aburdene. Even if managers comprehend the language of people such as engineering specialists and systems designers, there are simply too few lay managers to review every technical decision made by experts or even general decisions made by their own workers. Managers who attempt to monitor all decisions often fall victim to stress or burnout.

Finally, responding to change requires a level of creativity that the traditional sanctions and incentives—threats of demotion or firing—just cannot produce. Companies used to believe they had to frustrate individual initiative in order to pursue the common good. "Faced by relatively routine problems," the organization man "was encouraged to seek routine answers," Toffler observed. "Unorthodoxy, creativity, venturesomeness were discouraged." In companies that make things happen today, however, employees are seen as the company's most important resource in meeting the challenge of change. Thus, creativity and innovativeness are not only valued, they are cultivated.

For all these reasons, distinctions between leaders and led are blurring. Ad-hoc task forces and teams are turning traditional tables of organization into dust-laden artifacts. Autocratic hierarchies are being sidestepped or scrapped. Today, in what Anthony terms the "Postindustrial Revolution," Naisbitt labels the "Information Age," and Toffler calls "Super-industrial Society," the new style of management is **participation.**

In the participative environment "managers actually share their authority and power for decision making," Anthony explains. "The subordinates have meaningful input and the decision is made as a team. . . . Managers are viewed as team leaders who lead with the best interests of themselves, their subordinates and the organization in mind." Naisbitt and Aburdene describe this shift as one "from the manager as order-giver to the manager as **facilitator.**"

Today rejection by management experts of authoritarian modes of management is almost universal. "The leader can no longer manage by Machiavellian techniques, which threaten and terrorize," comments Michael Maccoby. "There can no longer be management by power, by fear, or by status," agrees William J. Crockett. "The hierarchical structure where everyone has a superior and everyone has an inferior surely is corrupting of the human spirit—no matter how well it served us during the industrial period," say Naisbitt and Aburdene.

Then there are those who feel the autocratic style is just less practical. Leonard R. Sayles writes that "the typical method of instituting change in a hierarchy is an announcement tumbling down the line; it doesn't work, not because it is undemocratic but because it is inefficient. . . . With participation, trite as it may sound, the change becomes our change,' tailored in part to our needs and problems and not a resented foreign incursion into an already problematic workday.''

"We're not mounting this effort because it's a nice thing to do," confirms David Hanson, manager of GE's Ravenna, Ohio, plant. "Competitors all have money, technology, competence. The key then becomes how well you can motivate the people." Naisbitt and Aburdene agree that "It is not a question of being nice to people. *It is simply a recognition that human beings can make or break a company.*"

Wide Spread Acceptance of the Concept of Participation

The concept of employee participation has taken hold so firmly that it is hard to find a current book about management that doesn't either promote participation or assume it. Given the trends in the marketplace and the workforce, participation is widely acknowledged as the way of the future. The benefits ascribed to it are numerous.

Marshall Sashkin observes that participation alleviates feelings of powerlessness and meaninglessness that have plagued workers since the Industrial Revolution. "As people mature, a basic human need for autonomy and control over one's own behavior emerges as part of the natural process of development," Sashkin observes. "While it cannot be suggested that participation in goal setting and decision making will magically and totally remedy workers' feelings of powerlessness . . . sound evidence indicates that participative management approaches involving goal setting and decision making do increase workers' sense of power and control."

Concerning the sense of meaninglessness engendered by the splitting up of jobs into small repetitive tasks, Sashkin writes, "The very structure of the human brain seems to press individuals to achieve a sense of completion or closure with respect to perceptions, tasks, and activities. . . . It is not surprising, then, that the problem of meaningless work is alleviated when workers engage participatively in solving problems and creating changes."

Dr. Alex Cohen of the National Institute of Occupational Health and Safety and Dr. Paul Rosch of the American Institute of Stress say that by eliminating powerlessness or "a lack of personal recognition and control over one's destiny at work," participation also reduces stress, which costs American industry as much as $100 million a year in absenteeism, reduced productivity and medical fees.

The Manager as Facilitator

Complementing the many descriptions and endorsements of participation are the multitude of books and articles portraying the qualities and skills of the manager of the participative environment.

"We used to think that the manager's job was to know all the answers," say Naisbitt and Aburdene. "But in the 1980s, the new manager ought, rather, to know the questions, to be concerned about them and involve others in finding answers. Today's manager needs to be more of a facilitator—someone skilled in eliciting answers from others, perhaps from people who do not even know that they know. . . .

"People cannot be supervised into getting it right. They have to bring the spirit of getting it right with them to the job."

Robert H. Hayes of Harvard Business School writes in the *New York Times* that "the role of top management is not to spot and solve problems as much as to create an organization that can spot and solve its own problems." Rather than "the leader who solves all problems," agrees Michael Maccoby, "we need leaders who encourage us to solve them together."

The facilitator's role therefore is to lead the group in drawing out answers, building a vision and developing plans that motivate everybody to achieve agreed upon goals—in short, to win. The more input the manager collects and channels, the more creativity is released.

The facilitator functions much like the conductor of a symphony, orchestrating and bringing forth the talents and contributions of others.

The facilitator is also a communicator. Working with decentralized structures such as networks, small teams and cross-departmental task forces—which more firms are embracing as alternatives to the corporate hierarchy—the facilitator fosters communication and understanding between the units.

Paul R. Lawrence captures the spirit of this new approach in writing in the *Harvard Business Review:* "Do managers think of their duties primarily as checking up, delegating and following through, applying pressure when performance fails to measure up? Or do they think of them primarily as facilitating communication and understanding between people with different points of view—for example, between a staff engineering group and a production group who do not see eye to eye on a change they are both involved in? An analysis of management's actual experience points to the latter as the more effective concept of administration."

Naisbitt and Aburdene refer to that as "a networking style of management, where people learn from one another horizontally, where everyone is a resource for everyone else, and where each person gets support and assistance from many different directions." Likewise, William H. Peace notes in the *Harvard Business Review,* that "frequent, thorough, open communication to every employee is essential . . . to keep walls from building within the company."

The facilitator also promotes continual learning within the organization. Naisbitt and Aburdene write, "We have to think about the manager as teacher, as mentor, as developer of human potential. Inside the corporation, the manager's new role will be to cultivate a nourishing environment for personal growth." According to Peter Senge of Innovation Associates, "the leader is ultimately responsible for the organizational learning process."

The Facilitator as Leader

The word leader has cropped up again and again in surveying the facilitator's role. This is because, perhaps above all else, people want to be led, not managed. The distinction is drawn by John H. Zenger in an article in *Training* magazine called "Leadership: Management's Better Half":

"If we define management as the administrative ordering of things—with written plans, clear organization charts, well-documented annual objectives, frequent reports, detailed and precise position descriptions and regular evaluations of performance against objectives—then it is true that many organizations are well-managed. . . . Leaders, on the other hand, provide visionary inspiration, motivation and direction. Leadership generates an emotional connection between the leader and the led. Leadership attracts people and inspires them to put forth incredible efforts in a common cause."

Groups without leaders tend to meander. Groups with Prussian-style autocrats instead of leaders rebel, quit or work just hard enough to keep their paychecks coming. Groups with true leaders, though, act as a team and are motivated to use their own creativity to meet any challenge.

James MacGregor Burns concludes that "the goal of a leader is not to exert force, but to 'empower' his or her followers; leaders are more like holy men than muscle men." This style of leadership, coupled with the participative style of management, empowers not just the followers, but the organization itself.

The idea of participation is not new. Nor is it untried. Nevertheless, it is sadly underused in today's corporations, despite the accolades from leading management experts. While competition in the marketplace requires the utmost in creativity, productivity and teamwork from workers, while workers demand greater responsibility and development of their skills, and while organizations are undergoing metamorphosis in response to these pressures, few managers seem to recognize that the best way to achieve that transformation is through participation.

CHAPTER 2

A Crisis in Participation

THE HUGHES TOOL STORY

When managers of Hughes Tool Company of Houston, Texas, decided to venture into a whole new product line in the late sixties, they became convinced that they would also need a new style of management to accompany it. The plan to manufacture tungsten carbide for rock bits was a major move into one of industry's most demanding and complex products. Setting up such an operation from scratch and developing the specifications, technology and manufacturing processes would take a high level of teamwork to succeed.

The company established a new division, the Powder Metals Group, and commissioned J. R. Whanger to lead the group through its bold new pioneering venture in participative management. Whanger knew it would not be easy. He knew that it would take time for employees to shift from old familiar patterns. At the same time, Whanger recalls that people were ready for a change. He knew even at that early date that fewer and fewer employees regarded themselves as "ones who just follow orders."

Whanger also knew that such wide-sweeping change would have to start from and be assimilated at the top, if there was any hope of its working at lower levels of the organization. Whanger used new methods of self-management intensively with a key group of division supervisors before attempting to use the new approach with hourly workers. His goal was to accustom these supervisors to "teamwork, group problem-solving and consensus decision-making" before involving others.

Four structures became the "pillars" of the Powder Metals Group's operations:

1. annual planning sessions,
2. monthly staff meetings,

15

3. problem solving sessions, and
4. guild circles.

Annual planning sessions were built around a new format, designed to deeply involve the group in creating an overall picture. At these gatherings everyone participated in formulating the vision of the division's future. Together they identified the obstacles they would have to overcome together, created their strategic directions and specified tactics and timetables for implementation.

Whanger found that this got immediate results:

> A widely diffused sense of responsibility developed in the Powder Metals Group. I attribute it to the fact that the Group's vision was developed together and was agreed upon in open meetings. This was more than communication; it was management by consensus. Not only did we get better decisions, but a commitment was made by all to carry out the decisions.

Following the annual planning were **monthly staff meetings** with all the salaried personnel, again using a set of procedures that ensured full participation. Whanger insisted that these meetings have a double intent: 1) gaining a comprehensive perspective of the company and the industry and 2) focusing group awareness on specific issues or necessary planning around projects and issues.

> The purpose was to get everyone to see the big picture and how their activity fit in. The first sign of success was the elimination of shift-to-shift bickering and finger-pointing. The next was when problems began to be resolved at the floor level before they became big problems.

A third structure introduced into the operations, the **problem-solving sessions**, also used a teamwork approach. These sessions were held whenever an issue arose that required getting a few heads together around the table. Again, they followed a consensus process and included follow-up schedules and an accountability structure. "More than once," Whanger says, this process "allowed us to hurdle problems that could have become serious."

As supervisors saw the results of the self-management process within their group, they became believers. They became skilled in using the new approach and began to communicate principles and methods of participative management within their own groups. At this point, the fourth component, **guild circles** were implemented with the hourly workers. Whanger is quick to point out that these were quite different from the quality circles that were later to gain popularity in American manufacturing.

The guild circles were shorter versions of the annual planning sessions. They followed the same procedural steps under the premise that workers within a department constituted a team to get a job done. Unlike quality circles, Whanger emphasizes, this program "was more comprehensive, in that it was as much people-oriented as product-oriented. A powerful influence was the inclusion of the **Vision Workshop**. This was a step beyond just utilizing a worker's knowledge of the job."

At first, a few workers used the circles as complaint sessions. This stopped as people recognized them as opportunities to actually participate in designing their future. Most employees developed a deep interest in working together to improve things and brought enough peer pressure on the others that everyone soon began to work as a team.

Two things surprised many supervisors. First was that the organizational vision that the hourly workers came up with was nearly identical to the one the supervisors themselves had created. Instead of pushing for lower production standards or better pay, as some supervisors had expected, the workers focused on how to ensure the operation's success, upgrade equipment, improve communications and train for expanded responsibilities.

The other surprise was the effect of the circles on the foremen. As Whanger puts it,

> The experience of leading the circles helped them work together among themselves and with the other salaried staff. It was like they saw clearly for the first time the whole picture of a human workforce running well. They really experienced leadership and the meaning of being part of a group with a goal. Their sense of involvement moved to another level.

Hughes' experiment became a dramatic success. The Powder Metals Group accomplished its immediate goals of developing new technology, building a fully integrated plant and manufacturing a new precision product line. But over the years, participative management has also enabled production at high volumes, achieving a productivity index of 110 percent; consistent on-time delivery of products; an exceptional safety record for the industry and finally, an extremely low absentee rate. Furthermore, Hughes has also enjoyed remarkably cooperative union relations. Whanger sums it up:

> This has been going on for over ten years now, so it is a time-tested project in the real world with typical production workers. Nor were the supervisors any kind of specially selected people. They were mostly (75%) chosen from the hourly workers assigned to Powder Metals. There were no factors that would keep what happened in Powder Metals from being repeated in other shops.

> We intended the workers' groups to give us some bright innovations, some straightforward good ideas to improve shop operations, and we got them. But the greatest improvement was in the spirit and attitude of the shop as a whole. I could tell it the minute I walked in. People would grab me and want to talk about what they were doing. We became a team.

Breaking Down the Barriers

There are several barriers that prevent managers from adopting the participative approach to management. Many new learnings about participation are now available from those who have adopted it. The barriers threaten the growth of participation, while the learnings provide new opportunities for enhancing both the breadth and depth of its use. In

Chinese characters, the combination of "threat" and "opportunity" constitutes the word "crisis." Today there is a crisis in participation.

Barriers that prevent managers from adopting a participative approach fall into three major categories:

1. managers are afraid of losing their power or control,
2. they are unclear about how to put participation into practice, or
3. they have been burned by earlier unsuccessful attempts at participative management.

The managers and the employees at Hughes Tool faced and overcame each of the major barriers to participation. This does not mean that these barriers are not real or that they are easily overcome. Nevertheless, they can be, and have been, surmounted by management experts and by the brave souls who have risked confronting them.

Fear of Loss of Power or Control

Many managers resist participation because they fear it will erode their power. "The failure or refusal at many organizations to make the necessary conversion [to a participative approach]," writes Bill Saporito in *Fortune,* "is hung up on old issues of authority." Such authority remains a clear badge of rank to many managers, for whom the idea of participation still doesn't sit right. William P. Anthony agrees that many managers think participation is "a management style that has little power or influence over subordinates. They feel that they will lose control and that subordinates will run roughshod over them."

Such fear of losing power often results from a conscious or unconscious distrust of subordinates. This manifests itself in several ways.

One manifestation of distrust is a belief harbored by some managers that participation must be accompanied or succeeded by chaos and anarchy. Such fear expressed by supervisors at Hughes Tool's Powder Metals Group eventually proved groundless.

Whanger recalls that his foremen were reluctant to even leave the factory floor to attend a scheduled meeting for fear that the hourly workers would stop work and just sit around smoking while supervisors were gone. Whanger persisted, however, and while the foremen were in their meeting the operations of the shift went on as usual. The only harm done in the supervisors' absence was to their own egos when they realized that their controlling presence wasn't as indispensable as they had thought.

Some managers worry that employees will be selfish, putting their own welfare ahead of the company's bottom line.

But managers at Hughes Tool discovered that employees tend to share the same visions as their bosses when allowed to share in their own company's destiny. Expected to argue for better pay and lower standards, employees instead urged improvements in product quality and production efficiency. Only tangentially did Hughes employees even bring up the matter of their working conditions. When the managers put those suggestions into action, the workers felt that the managers really cared about them, elevating employee trust of their supervisors. That engendered better communication and a new spirit of team-work.

Many other companies have had similar experiences. Research reported by Sashkin adds further support to the efficacy of participative systems. Sashkin says studies have proved that: ''(1) goals that are participatively set are higher than those that are set for a person by others (that is, 'assigned') and (2) higher (more difficult) goals result in higher levels of performance.'' A survey by the U.S. Chamber of Commerce also found that 84% of American workers said they'd actually work harder if they were given the right to take part in making decisions. This evidence reveals that, given the opportunity to participate in making corporate decisions, employees' sense of responsibility is enlarged.

A few managers object that participation means decisions will be made by ''uninformed'' employees. This is dangerous arrogance. The whole idea behind participation is that the real experts are the people involved from day to day in getting the job done. In solving a problem on the production line, or revamping the operations of a department, or even setting the five-year strategy of an entire corporation, the people most involved are the ones who know best what will or won't work. To forge a decision that is well-informed and practical, a manager must tap the wisdom of the people who are most directly related to the issue from as many perspectives as possible.

Hughes Tool's experience reveals yet another dimension of the fear of losing power or control. Whanger refers to ''islands of resistance'' to participation, found to be most inflexible among middle management.

> Our experience is that middle management seems to be the group that has the most entrenched, standpat people. That may be because most middle managers have gotten to their position by being successful in the old manner of things and worry that a change could wipe out their field of expertise. It's not that they don't know it's good to use the knowledge of workers but that they think their own importance could be reduced.

Recalling the incident when the foremen expressed surprise that employees stayed busy at their jobs while they were absent in a meeting, Whanger suspects that some of the foremen were disappointed.

> They had seen themselves as the ones who had to drive the group to perform. Now their self image was at stake. Their reason for existence had been shaken.

> Another effect on middle managers was that after the workers' program was operating, the workers began pushing for results on their proposals. Since the foreman is the management person closest to the workforce, he heard about it often. Of course, the foremen are always getting pressure from higher management to show results. Now they were also getting it from below and they were caught in a squeeze.

> What could be better for a results-oriented company than having all levels of your organization promoting positive action? It was a good situation if the foremen were prepared for it, but if not, they could find it intolerable.

The question was how to get middle management to see the participative groups in a favorable way. The method that worked was to start with participatory groups among the foremen so that they recognized it would be successful. So before starting a participatory program with the worker level people, we did a similar program with the foremen. By the time we moved to the shop worker level, the foremen were absolutely sold on the program.

Next, Whanger and his colleagues trained the foremen to lead the hourly workers' meetings. "We made it the foremen's program," he says. "That way, they see that they don't lose power and the push from below demonstrates their own success. So middle management (foremen in our case) is the key."

Saporito reports similar results elsewhere. When Boeing initiated a participative program in 1984, for example, "middle managers failed to support the effort because they were left out of it. . . . Only when the middle managers were invited into the program did it begin to take off, resulting in . . . a 400% return on the money invested in setting it up."

To fears of losing power and control, Anthony responds,

Just because managers share their authority and power does not mean they have any less of it. Power and authority are not fixed, finite qualities. When managers and subordinates share authority, a synergistic effect occurs. . . . The actions of the manager and the group working together under a common basis of shared authority creates greater authority than the manager exercising authority alone. . . .

Since the total authority level is increased through this synergistic effect, the power of the group relative to others in the organization is also increased. . . . If all managers and subordinates in the organization work as teams, the organization as a whole will have more power in relation to organizations with which it must deal.

So contrary to the belief of many a manager, participation can actually increase the authority, power, and influence of managers and their groups, not weaken it."

Participation increases the power of managers, the power of workers and the welfare of the company. Everyone wins.

Ambiguity About How to put Participation to Work

A second major barrier to participation, Marshall Sashkin says, is that most managers are unclear as to what participative management is all about.

American business schools graduate over 50,000 MBAs every year. In both their graduate and undergraduate business education, most of these students are taught the value of participative management. Yet, despite the educational exposure and emphasis, American managers do not, in general, seem to employ participative management approaches. While many seem familiar with the catchwords and jargon of participative management, few seem to be able to turn these phrases into managerial behaviors. . . . Most managers probably avoid participative management methods simply because they do not know what the specific methods are, how they work, or what situations to use them in.

Because of such uncertainty some managers are unwilling to climb out of familiar management ruts, unwilling to make the effort to change their way of operating. They may be unwilling to cast aside the security blanket of the traditional style to try something new. Or they may not believe it's necessary.

"Managers who think that their businesses are producing acceptable results," writes Bill Saporito, "aren't particularly interested in changing their ways." He notes the feeling that this "if-it-ain't-broke-don't-fix-it" notion may be holding back U.S. management.

Sashkin concludes that "both research and practice clearly indicate that participative approaches do yield improved performance and productivity." He also notes that "effective application of participative management is very likely (about a 95 percent chance) to result in a minimum 15 percent improvement in hard measures of performance and productivity." Why then, should managers settle for the status quo; particularly in a world of rapidly escalating competition; in a world where tomorrow might bring unexpected dangers that could threaten their very own corporate survival?

"In technology, we expect bold experiments that test ideas, obtain new knowledge, and lead to major advances," Jay Forrester comments. "But in matters of social organization, we usually propose only timid modifications of conventional practice and balk at daring experiment and innovation."

It is our hope that this book will help overcome this barrier. By laying out step-by-step procedures of a system called the *Technology of Participation (ToP)*, as well as illustrations of various applications in different situations, we hope that managers will be encouraged to try these techniques, learning as they go. Like any skill, prowess in managing participation grows with practice.

Discouragement From Earlier Attempts at Participation

Some managers fear participative management will fail because previous attempts at employee participation, such as quality circles and similar isolated efforts did not produce the expected results. But it is important to distinguish that quality circles are only one small example of participative management. Still, QCs are often times the first exposure people have to participative planning. It is worth examining, therefore, some of the factors that can undermine their effectiveness.

Saporito attributes "not the workers but management—upper, middle and lower," as the major reason for the failure of quality circles. "The concept was banished to the shop floor, and even if it flourished there, was never permitted to climb higher. Jump on the quality circle bandwagon? Sure, takers were everywhere. But change the behavior of managers or the organizational structure? Not this decade, thanks."

Worse than merely banishing QC's to the shop floor, some managers adopted these circles merely as an attempt to placate employees and perhaps to short-circuit their grievances. Such managers never really intended to heed workers' suggestions. "Many chief executives preach the virtues of employee involvement, teamwork and participative management," the *New York Times* reports, "but for a calculated reason. Personnel cutbacks have taken a heavy toll on employee loyalty, which, in turn, threatens to take a toll on company efforts to bolster productivity and product quality. As a consequence, executives face the difficult paradox of having to convince employees that they really care about them—until the axe falls in the next wave of cutbacks."

Such lip service, or superficial programs are doomed to fail. They may even backfire on the supervisors. Anthony explains that "it can lower morale severely and may have other deleterious consequences if the employees think their suggestions are being taken seriously when they are not. The employees can feel they have been taken in and hoodwinked. They may think it is all a big game . . . "

William H. Peace justifies such concern in a story of quality circle failure in the *Harvard Business Review.* "My staff and I . . . had waffled months before when the engineers' quality circle made design recommendations for an office building that was nearly complete. Rather than tell the group, which included a contingent of bright, vocal and aggressive professionals, that it was too late to accept any changes (or else prepare ourselves for some expensive last-minute redesign), we let them put forth their ideas and then shot them down. The office was completed on time and on budget, but the quality circle broke up and the employees had continuing reason to dislike their offices and mistrust management."

Sashkin offers another reason many quality circles fail: ". . . the rapid spread of the QC approach has often resulted in poor-quality implementation of participative group problem solving by trainers and consultants who neither fully understand the approach nor have the skills needed to effectively train people to use it. . . . The failure to provide such high-quality training may ultimately create a backlash from managers against the QC approach, when these inadequate 'installations' begin to result in failures."

Still another problem pointed out by Mitchell Lee Marks in an article in *Psychology Today,* lies in the nature of delegation. "People who propose the changes are usually not the ones who actually implement them." Citing a study conducted by a team from the University of Southern California (USC) Center for Effective Organization, Marks reports that, "in many cases, the change is not implemented well, is not implemented at all, or is implemented and just does not save the money projected." Such implementation problems lead Marks to conclude that quality circles are like aspirin: "They treat symptoms and provide some immediate relief but don't touch the underlying issues of management-employee tensions, lack of respect and underutilization that cause the problems in the first place."

Quality circles have worked well at the level at which they are applied, provided they are applied carefully by well-trained leaders and are effectively followed through. Unfortunately, this often doesn't happen. Even when they are applied effectively, their intent is generally focused, rather than comprehensive. They cannot be expected to solve all of an organization's problems.

The USC study's three recommendations of effective ways to use quality circles include one that states, "QC's may help in making the transition to more participative management systems."

Susan A. Mohrman of the USC research team observes that the QC approach simply "does not go far enough, it is not strong enough to promote real organizational change. For that, you need to go further and rethink the design of jobs, decision making processes and organizational structures."

Such pervasive organizational change is, in fact, being recognized by more and more companies every day as the key to survival in an ever-changing marketplace and with a more demanding workforce. While participation has been acknowledged as the best approach for bringing about such organizational transformation, it cannot be done by participation in the old, limited sense of the word.

What then is required of organizations, of managers and of participation today?

A New Understanding of Participation is Emerging

Despite problems and frustrations with attempts at participative management, participation has come of age. Managers who are genuinely interested in participative techniques are no longer looking for a program. Enlightened by news of experiments, failures and successes in this new management technique, they now seek a system, even an environment. They have learned, mostly by hard experience, that there are no "quick fixes" for improving employee motivation and productivity.

Our experience in working with thousands of organizations all over the world has revealed that a new understanding of participation is emerging. This new understanding can be broken down into four basic tenets:

1. Participation is an ongoing, integrated, whole-system approach.

2. Participation is an evolving, organic and dynamic process.

3. Participation is a structured process involving learnable skills.

4. Participation requires a commitment to openness from everyone involved.

1. Participation is an ongoing, integrated, whole-system approach.

If full benefits are to be realized, this system cannot be applied to an isolated team or department within an organization.

Participation is not just "a gewgaw bolted onto the management machinery by social engineers," as Saporito says many firms have done. Nor is it "installed," as if it were a muffler on a car, as Sashkin says quality circles often are. Thomas McKenna of Midwest Steel concludes that true participation "is not a program. It is a whole different way of dealing with people." Introducing participation into an organization's operations does not add something new—it transforms the existing mode of operation.

2. Participation is an evolving, organic and dynamic process.

It is not a one-shot, quick-fix program. Neglected, it will wither away or even backfire. Nurtured, it will grow and enhance the entire corporate culture with cooperation, team spirit, creativity and motivation.

Obviously, there must be a starting point. At Eaton, the top 150 executives were trained in participative techniques. At Hughes Tool, the foremen spent two years practicing participative methods before introducing them to the shop floor. With encouragement, the style and spirit will spread throughout the organization. If it is stifled, however, or confined to a certain level within the organization, it is likely to poison relations between workers and management in a fashion similar to Peace's experience.

3. Participation is a structured process involving learnable skills.

It is freedom within a framework. Managing participation is a discipline that can be learned, not a charisma born to some people and not to others.

Participative-type freedom "is not the absence of structure—letting employees go off and do whatever they want", writes Rosabeth Moss Kanter in *The Change Masters,* "but rather a clear structure which enables people to work within established boundaries in an autonomous and creative way." Whanger of Hughes Tool agrees. He describes some managers who normally are strong leaders with personable style, who attempt to lead meetings with their workers without a plan or a structure. "I have seen some very capable managers have dismal experiences attempting this. . . . The proper method is a most valuable tool that has wide usage. . . . A thorough understanding of its usage is the beginning step in facilitator training."

4. Participation requires a commitment to openness from everyone involved.

Operating modes and values will be changed. For some, these changes will come easily, but for others, they will be painfully difficult. Still, learning to remain open to change and to take an active role in shaping change can be a most valuable lesson for our times.

Larry Wilson, founder of Wilson Learning, underscores the need to become a learning organization. "Things that used to work in education, business, government and religious institutions are no longer effective. Things are entirely different. . . . We are in an era in which fundamental values are changing, expectations are changing and the process of how-to is changing. . . . These are times for living between trapezes. . . . We have to let go of what we've done before, of what doesn't work, and learn to live with ambiguity while we find something better."

As more and more organizations recognize the need to change their operational style and their organizational structure in response to change, they are discovering that participation is a critical component of the new culture they seek to develop. "Vehicles for greater participation at all levels are an important part of an innovating company," writes Kanter. "Masters of Change are also masters of the use of participation."

In the following chapters we will look at several specific methods of participation that comprise the *Technology of Participation*. How these methods can help achieve management objectives will be discussed through numerous case studies supplied by clients and associates who have applied *ToP* methods to solving their organizations' problems.

PART TWO

The Methods of the *Technology of Participation*

CHAPTER 3

The Texaco Story

The *Technology of Participation (ToP)* is comprised of several basic group facilitation techniques which can be applied to important organization and management tasks. At the core of *ToP* are specific methods and skills which will be described in detail in Chapters 4, 5 and 6. Specific applications of *ToP* to meet certain needs will be described in Part III. The following case study provides an overview of the *ToP* process and its results. This study involves the *Strategic Planning Process*, one of the most popular applications of *ToP*.

* * *

At a mountain retreat in the interior of Jamaica, managers and key retailers from Texaco, Inc. met to evaluate their unit's future. In five years this regional unit of Texaco had plummetted from first to last among the region's three distributors, and from 42% to 11.7% in market share. The company's relationships with retailers had soured, numerous major accounts had been lost, and two thirds of its corporate staff had been dismissed. The new general manager, Bob Harper, was a marketing expert. His orders from headquarters were succinct. "Either shape up the operation or shut it down."

Harper wasn't one to back away from a crisis. He chose to begin his unit's climb back to the top by applying *ToP*. To accomplish this, he had contracted with the Institute of Cultural Affairs for a *ToP Strategic Planning Session*.

The session was just getting underway.

Mapping out a Practical Vision

The facilitator stood next to a chalkboard bearing the theme, or focus question for the seminar: "How can the Texaco family regain its regional leadership position as providers of top quality consumer service?"

Now the facilitator turned to the participants, seated at tables in a semicircle facing him. He straightened his necktie and spoke:

"Imagine it is five years in the future. You are reading a feature article on the success of your organization. What does the article highlight about your success? What does it say about the uniqueness of your organization? What services does it report that you are providing? What does it tell about how you've changed in the past five years?

"Given the stated area of concern, 'regaining Texaco's leadership position as providers of top quality consumer service,' what is the recognizable condition you would hope to have in place in the next five years?"

Before he could concentrate on a vision of the future, several thoughts about the past crowded Bob Harper's mind.

First, and Harper smiled at the thought, just getting the retailers and executives together in the same room was a major accomplishment. Years of pent-up frustration had led to a gap created by a "we-they" mentality between the regional office and the retailers. That gap had become Texaco's biggest stumbling block.

Harper brought *ToP* into the picture after acquaintances on the ICA staff familiarized him with previous *ToP* induced victories. It was ICA staff that encouraged Harper to gather office staff and retailers together as the Texaco "family" to begin with. Sparking even more interest, the ICA showed Harper an article detailing the success of the Total Market Approach (TMA) at McDonald's. Franchise owners and marketing officials there had gained a new sense of teamwork, translating directly into increased sales, through the use of *ToP* methods.

ICA facilitators moderated preliminary talks between Texaco's office staff and retailers. Those talks were necessary to even persuade retailers to attend the session. The talks included a *Design Conference* conducted by the ICA to map out a program tailored to Texaco's particular needs, and to draw up a session theme—the *focus question*. The *Design Conference* gave Harper a chance to lay out the harsh figures showing Texaco's dramatic decline in market share. That shocked the retailers into realizing that "we're all in this together." The realization also allowed the retailers to offer ideas about the focus question. They began to understand that, in large part, the event would be their own. They would help shape Texaco's new marketing plan.

Harper gritted his teeth, however, as he recalled that even then the retailers almost didn't show up. "What a legacy of repressed anger, though some of it was certainly justified," he mused. Earlier that day key retailers had threatened to boycott the program. Again the ICA facilitators had stepped into the breech, reminding the retailers that a plan built without their input would be worthless. After several hours of noisy debate, everyone attended the meeting.

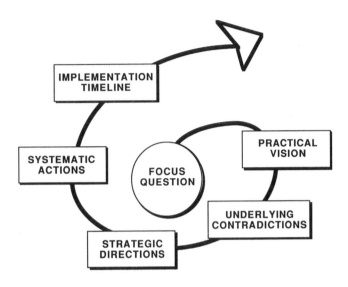

"A vision of the future," Harper thought. "Sure, everyone working together in harmony, that's mine. But is that hoping for a miracle?"

According to the facilitators, it wasn't. They had explained to Harper that participatory planning with *ToP* had proven effective in all kinds of organizations in over forty countries. "The process bridges the gap between theory and practice," one of the staff told him, "between the way things are and the way you want them to be." In Texaco's case that was a very wide chasm to bridge.

Harper's eyes wandered for a moment to a diagram at the front of the room.

He was viewing an outline of the seminar's five steps. He recalled from earlier discussions that the diagram's spiral signifies a continually ongoing and expanding process, one that adapts to changes as often as necessary.

The ICA staff had explained to Harper that the five stage process could be scheduled over two, three or four days. It could involve any or all segments of the company—from top management and board of trustees down to hourly staff. The process could work with groups of four to four hundred people, and would culminate in a written *action plan* targeted to the specific needs of the organization.

Most of all, they added, the process allows an organization to step back from the hustle and bustle of its daily operations and examine its long-term directions in a brief and concentrated period of time.

The ICA facilitator, Sherwood Shankland, had started the seminar with a round of introductions, followed by an exercise called a "trends conversation." Participants took turns recalling recent world, national and company trends and events. By creating a common perspective of Texaco's current situation in light of recent world and regional history, the trends conversation set the stage for shaping a common vision of the company's future.

Harper noted that Shankland was performing the role he had said he would, that of a facilitator rather than a consultant, guiding the discussion and eliciting the participation and insights of each member of the group so that the Texaco team would build the plan themselves.

"Maybe it's asking for a miracle," Harper said to the team as his own image of the future formed in his mind, "but I see Texaco once again being the very best distributor in the region . . ."

Shankland moved on to the next step. He asked the group to "list on the pad in front of you eight to ten elements of your vision, or conditions you'd like to see in place in the next five years that would regain Texaco's leadership position as providers of top quality consumer service."

"Now put a checkmark next to what you believe are the three best ideas on your list," Shankland said after a few minutes, "and regroup into teams of two with the person next to you. Each team will then select their best seven ideas, and write them in three-word phrases on the 5" x 8" cards I've passed out."

When the teams were finished writing, Shankland requested that each team "Choose from your cards the one that's clearest, or easiest to understand and pass it to me." After collecting the cards, he posed questions to clarify some of the phrases, while his co-facilitator, Ellen Rebstock, taped the cards at random on the front wall.

Next Shankland called for the card "most crucial to consumer service."

As Rebstock placed the cards on the wall, Shankland asked "what cards seem to go together?" Rebstock placed those cards in vertical columns according to the participants' replies.

Then Shankland had the teams pass up "the card that's most different from any so far," then, "the cards that fit into one of the columns we already have," and finally, "all the rest."

Shankland and the Texaco people then further refined the categories and assigned them precise titles. The composite vision included twelve clusters or themes grouped into three major sections.

THE PRACTICAL VISION

I TOWARDS A REVITALIZED CORPORATE IDENTITY		II TOWARDS CONSISTENT RELIABLE PERFORMANCE STANDARDS	III TOWARDS RECAPTURED MARKET SHARE AND FINANCIAL STRENGTH	
UNIFIED FAMILY IMAGE A	PUBLIC RELATIONS PROGRAMME B	C	DIVERSIFIED CUSTOMER SEVICE D	COMPETITIVE MARKET STRATEGIES E
BOLD CORPORATE IDENTITY 1	COMMUNITY INVOLVEMENT ACTIVITIES 3	PROFESSIONAL PERFORMANCE STANDARD 5 / COMPREHENSIVE TRAINING SERVICES 6	TOTAL SERVICE FACILITIES 9	FREE MARKET OPERATIONS 11
REGULAR INTERNAL COMMUNICATIONS 2	MULTI-MEDIA PROMOTION AND ADVERTISING 4	GUARANTEED PRODUCT INTEGRITY 7 / MODERNIZED FACILITY RENOVATIONS 8	EXPANDED PRODUCT LINES 10	CONSISTENT PRODUCT SUPPLIES 12

The cards taped on the wall under the title "Bold Corporate Identity" (number 1), for example, were:

> Rehabilitated Retail Outlets
> Delivery Truck Identification
> Bold New Company Image
> —Uniforms
> —Store Appearance
> Company/Family Leadership Image

"Regular Internal Communications" (number 2) included:

> Monthly Newsletters
> Quarterly Retailer Plan
> Texaco Family Unification
> Scheduled Representative Contact
> Regular Planning Sessions

The list continued in that fashion.

After the cards had been organized and posted, Shankland turned toward the group, and asked: "Now what would happen if all of these ideas went into effect?"

"We'd be the best distributor in the region," someone declared. Heads nodded in agreement among the participants.

As the group filed out for lunch, Harper thought to himself, "It seems less like a miracle all the time." Some of his earlier doubts were vanishing.

Analyzing Underlying Contradictions

The Texaco team returned from lunch ready to take on stage two of the *Strategic Planning Process*. That involved **Analyzing Underlying Contradictions**.

Having looked into the future and welded a common vision, participants were now prepared to tackle obstacles that might block that vision. The reasons for their lingering mistrust, which had already begun to fade away, were finally about to be confronted.

When all the participants were seated, Ellen Rebstock pointed to the columns of vision cards taped to the front wall and asked: "What are the issues, obstacles, constraints or barriers, that could prevent this vision from becoming a reality?"

Rebstock asked each member of the group to address that question by jotting down ideas and observations, at least one for each of the 12 components of the vision. Those ideas were to be specific rather than abstract. They were to be objective realities, based on actual experience or first-hand knowledge, rather than subjective feelings. The participants scribbled on their note pads for about five minutes.

The task done, Rebstock had them pair off in teams of two. She asked each team to select five or six of their best ideas and write them down on cards. She then asked each team to pass forward the card that was the easiest to understand. Cards with notations like "misallocation of time," "negative internal rivalry," "limited manpower resources," "dormant sales personnel," and "top-down policy making" were passed to the front of the room.

Again the clarifying process began. Rebstock asked questions to clarify the comments as Shankland taped the cards to the wall. Bob Harper felt tense. "Any moment now," he thought, "shouts will break out from all sides and this meeting will degenerate into a free-for-all."

When he looked around, though, everyone seemed reasonably calm. He'd expected a near riot. But what he saw was near-total cooperation. As Rebstock called for "a card picked at random," and then "a card that's a little different," Harper relaxed again.

Now Rebstock asked the Texaco people to decide what cards seemed to go together, just as they had in the vision stage. She grouped those cards into clusters according to the responses. Then the teams passed up any cards that fit into an already existing category, followed by the remaining cards that didn't seem to fit anywhere.

THE UNDERLYING CONTRADICTIONS

I NON-PARTICIPATORY INSENSITIVE MANAGEMENT STYLE	II INAPPROPRIATE ALLOCATION & USE OF RETAIL FACILITY IMPROVEMENT FUNDS	III LOW CORPORATE PRIORITY FOR INTERNATIONAL ADVERTISING	IV POLARIZED RELATIONSHIP REFLECTED IN NEGATIVE PERSONAL ATTITUDES	V UNIDENTIFIED CORPORATE IDENTITY	VI INADEQUATE TRAINING RESOURCES AND PROGRAMMES	VII ONEROUS GOVERNMENT FISCAL POLICY	VIII INSUFFICIENT KNOWLEDGE OF PRODUCTS & SERVICES	IX ADVERSE EFFECT OF KEROSENE SUBSIDY ON PRODUCT QUALITY	X THREAT OF UNFAIR GOVERNMENT (MARKETING) COMPETITION
Misallocation of time	Unavailable equipment spares	Unbudgeted public relations campaign	Negative internal rivalry	Undefined corporate identity	Undefined training resources	Government regulation	Limited manpower resources	Subsidized kero price	Direct government involvement
Neglect by people in management	Obsolete equipment	Undelivered standards accountability	Weak communication link	Neglecting projection of Texaco image	Dormant sales personnel	Unavailibility of product line	Consumers don't see product benefits	Inconsistent product quality	
Top-down policymaking	Insecure station building structure	Unperceived benefits of advertisement	Communications structure breakdown	Undefined quality image	Discontinues standards compliance	High interest rates - Exchange controls	Unawareness of Texaco services	Impotent government quality control	
Insufficient forward planning	Un-utilized facilities	Unappreciated culture involvement	Resistance to change	Un-implemented performance standards	Low training priority	Uncompetitive product pricing			
Liaison with Marketer-Dealer	Workmanship & maintenance of station	Unaware of need for public relations upgrading	Retailer resistance to change	Unidentified community resources	Inadequate staff/retailer/attendant training	High import duty			
Low identification with the local "JA"	Inconsistent station design & appearance	Zero advertising effort	Poor driver retailer relationship	Individualistic approach to corporate identity					
No competitive spirit	Neglected appearance of stations	Community involvement not to profit	Irresponsible delivery system						
Insecurity of goodwill	Funds improperly allocated (Maintenance)	Advertisement image as expenditure only	Discourteous attendants						
Sense of growth limitations	Inadequate retail facilities	Insufficient advertising budget							
Limited financial resources	Poor facility maintenance								
Not identified with Jamaica cause	Limited station space								
Operation oriented management	Inconsistent station rehabilitation								
12	12	9	8	6	5	5	3	3	1

When all the cards were in place, Rebstock pointed to each cluster and probed, "Now what's the root cause common to all of the cards in that section?" Those root causes became the titles of the sections.

The Texaco team had done well. They had identified 63 obstacles to their vision and divided them into 10 underlying contradictions. The section they'd titled "Inappropriate Allocation & Use of Retail Facility Improvement Funds," for instance, contained 12 items:

Unavailable Equipment Spares

Obsolete Equipment

Insecure Store Building Structure

Unutilized Facilities

Poor Workmanship & Maintenance of Stores

Inconsistent Store Design & Appearance

Neglected Appearance of Stores

Funds Improperly Allocated (Maintenance)

Inadequate Retail Facilities
Poor Facility Maintenance
Limited Store Space
Inconsistent Store Rehabilitation

This cluster had been potentially the most explosive issue among the retailers. Discussion here touched on what had long been the most volatile area of complaints. Yet the *ToP Strategic Planning Process* allowed those issues to be raised without rancor and without placing blame. By looking forward rather than backward, the process didn't permit finger pointing or singling out of culprits, even if there had been time for that.

Far from kindling anger, the exercise served as a kind of catharsis, relieving everybody's frustrations. By bringing those issues into the open, participants were able to get them off their chests. Contradictions or barriers that had been experienced by one faction or one person became the contradictions of the entire team. In the third stage of the process they would be confronted and resolved by the team.

Setting Strategic Directions

The next morning the Texaco crew was back at the table, ready to begin the third stage of the process, called *Setting Strategic Directions*.

When everyone had settled in, Sherwood Shankland crossed the room and stood before the group. "Now is the time to be bold and creative," he said. "What new directions must we move toward in order to resolve the contradictions and realize our vision?" Shankland encouraged the group to focus on activities or programs that could be accomplished within the next three years.

Each participant was asked to list at least one general course of action for each of the ten contradictions identified the day before. Then teams of two chose their five or six best suggestions and wrote them down on cards, following Shankland's instructions to strike a balance between venturesome and conservative actions.

Shankland next had the teams pass forward "the card that describes the boldest action," while Ellen Rebstock taped up the cards, and then "the card that's most conservative," and "the card that's most different from anything that's already up here." As in the previous stages, the cards were grouped into columns and given provisional names.

Next came the cards that fit into already existing groups, followed by the extras, to be merged with existing sections or arranged into columns of their own. Finally, all the columns were given appropriate titles.

It took the participants about two hours to draw up 16 arenas of strategic directions, split up into three major sections.

THE STRATEGIC DIRECTIONS

I TEXACO FAMILY MOTIVATION		II AGRESSIVE INTEGRATED MARKETING APPROACH	III RENEWED TEXACO IMAGE	
Effective Organization Communication A	*Ongoing Comprehensive Training* B	C	*Visible Retail Facility Transformation* D	*Coordinated Government Representation* E
Family Information and Planning System 1	Training School 3	Quality "Value" Dissemination 6	Phased Modernization Campaign 12	Equitable Public/Private Market Participation 15
		Technical Service Orientation 7		
	External Consumer Awareness Campaign 4	Family Incentives and Promotion 8	Consolidated Retail Network 13	
Internal Management Communications 2		Selective Credit Facilities 9		Favourable Lube Import Duty Review 16
	Company Internal Training Scheme 5	Gasoline Quality Assurance Strategy 10	Establish and Maintain Appearance Standards 14	
		Community Activities Participation 11		

As an example of the detail in each arena, the cards on the wall for number 6, "Quality Value Dissemination," were:

Establish Quality Service Guidelines

Establish Value of Quality in Texaco Products and Services

Product Resource Research (Locate Cheaper Sources)

"Community Activities Participation," number 11, consisted of:

Adopt Visible Community Project

Dynamic Social Involvement

Community Involvement Projects

Finally, framed within number 12, "Phased Modernization Campaign," were these strategic ideas:

Locally Manufactured Equipment

Retailer Participation (in Rehab Planning)

Rehab 20 Stores Annually

Shankland wrapped up the strategic directions stage by having the Texaco team reflect on which action arenas would be the easiest, the most difficult, and which would be the most exciting to implement. That conversation prepared the Texaco team for the fourth stage of the process, **Designing the Systematic Actions**.

As they left the room, participants were grinning and talking animatedly in small groups. Bob Harper was elated with the concepts, but still cautious about the outcome. "I'm not about to do cartwheels just yet. From time to time the boss has to play the devil's advocate. So I'm withholding judgment for now, until I see how all of those grand ideas are translated into plans. Still, I have to admit that it looks like the patient is going to pull through."

Many good business people are cautious, and Bob Harper is a good businessman. But as another business client, a bank officer in Illinois, said, "The highlight of the planning process for me was the transformation of vague ideas into specific actions—something you can really work with." In less than 24 hours, Bob Harper would become a true believer.

Designing the Systematic Actions

After lunch the group of Texaco staff and retailers returned to the meeting room, eager to tackle the next challenge. They now recognized that strategic directions are merely stepping stones leading to practical actions. It was practical action that would make their planned corporate future a reality.

"At last," Bob Harper remarked to his top marketing man, "we're getting down to the brass tacks." He would be surprised to find how sharp those tacks would prove to be.

Ellen Rebstock wrote on the chalkboard, in letters five inches high. It was seven minutes after one. The Texaco people watched as the words appeared one at a time: *What are the individual, measurable accomplishments that can be achieved by you to fulfill the strategic directions you have mapped out?*

As in the previous three sessions, small teams were formed to pool their ideas and select items to be sent to the front in response to Rebstock's questions: "Which action from your team's cards could be accomplished most quickly? . . ." "Which action would catalyze the greatest change or movement within the Texaco family? . . ." "Which action would have the broadest impact, addressing several contradictions at once?"

The cards were grouped into clusters, this time with other cards describing similar actions. As the group named each cluster of cards, Harper became excited by the concrete, hard-headed practicality of the planned sets of actions slowly taking shape on the board. He also became somewhat overwhelmed by the amount of work it would take to implement all of them. "Where would the people and the resources, let alone the time, come from to make all this happen?" he wondered. "It takes all our time, money and energy just to keep day-to-day operations going, and we're going down the tubes at that." At the same time, he could not isolate a single action posted on the board that was not vitally important

THE SYSTEMATIC ACTIONS

I. PROMOTING THE STORY OF THE RISING STAR				
	II. MAXIMIZING IMPLEMENTATION MEANS			
A. *Information* *Dissemination*	**B.** *Family* *Involvement*	**III. MARKETING** **DEVELOPMENT** **PROGRAMME**	**C.** *Resource* *Utilization*	**D.** *Comprehensive* *Enlightenment*
Update Information Resources 1	Establish Star Recognition Programmes 3	Design Advertisement Campaign 6	Local Manufacturing Facility 11	National Awareness and Education Campaign 14
		Developing Standards Criteria 7		
	Focusing Star Community Projects 4	Evaluate Financial Allocations 8	Engaging Appropriate Staff 12	
Structuring Interorganization Communication 2		Design Appropriate Facilities 9		Family Orientation Programme
	Annual Family Celebrations 5	Develop Q-Q Assurance Programme 10	Obtaining Adequate Financing 13	15

to implementing the plan the group had been building for the last two days—a plan of action which he was convinced would put Texaco back on top.

As if reading Harper's mind, Rebstock said, "Tomorrow morning, we will figure out what it will take to implement these actions. But it is pretty clear that we can't do all of them at once. We need to set priorities for them, in terms of urgency."

At this point, she put up a chart showing the next twelve months divided into quarters. She divided the group into three teams and assigned each team the task of establishing priorities for five actions. The teams were instructed to determine in which quarter of the coming year each action would be implemented, based on considerations such as "How urgent is this action?" "What has to happen before this action can be initiated?" and "Which actions would achieve quick, visible results that would generate momentum and catalyze more action in other areas?"

When the teams were finished, they wrote the name of each action on a card and placed that card on the chart in the quarter in which it would be implemented. The whole group then reviewed the timeline, asking questions for clarity and making changes where necessary.

When the timeline was completed and agreed upon, Rebstock led the group in a brief reflection on the session. Harper discovered that he was not alone in his feelings of excitement over the practicality of the planned actions or even in his sense of being overwhelmed by the work it would take to implement them. Others in the group were expressing the same sentiments. "When we began this process we were intimidated by the impossibility of it all," he thought to himself, But now we are overwhelmed by possibility and filled with excitement. And spreading these actions out over the year makes the job a bit less intimidating."

He sensed a shift in the group's attitude as they dispersed for dinner. There was a cockiness about them, a spirit of camaraderie and a readiness to take on any challenge. They reminded him of his soccer team when he was a youth. He remembered the spirit the team shared when getting ready for an important match.

Drawing up the Implementation Timeline

When the group entered the room the next morning, there was a new chart on the front wall. It was divided into three months and the weeks of each month. Down the side were listed eight actions, selected at the end of the previous day, for implementation in the next 90 days.

"This morning we will put wheels under our plan of action," said Sherwood Shankland. "We need to decide what steps will be required to implement each action, who will be responsible for seeing that those steps are taken, and when, where and how each step will be done.

"There are 24 members of the Texaco family represented here," he continued, "so we need about three volunteers to work on each action. I am not asking you to volunteer simply for the purpose of this exercise. I am asking you to take responsibility for the implementation of the action you choose."

> Harper was wary. The night before, he had consulted with Shankland and Rebstock on the best approach to this section of the process. They explained that assignments to work on the actions could be made arbitrarily, by "counting off," or Harper could make assignments based on what he knew of peoples' skills, propensities and interests. Or they could ask for volunteers and hope for adequate coverage of all the actions. There were advantages and risks in each approach, so they sought Harper's advice.

> Harper had weighed the options. Counting off seemed safe, he thought. Objectivity is always helpful. However, some people might get assigned to activities for which they had little interest. That might limit the energy and imagination that would go into the implementation plan.

> If he did the assigning himself, he could make sure he would get people with appropriate expertise in particular areas. On the other hand, that might inhibit fresh ideas from being introduced or certain members of the group might feel manipulated.

Finally, Harper chose the volunteer method, knowing that people would choose the area where they had the most interest and therefore would contribute the most energy. He was aware that this could lead to some great disparities—perhaps ten people would volunteer for one action and nobody would volunteer for several others. He decided to risk it when Shankland and Rebstock pointed out that those disparities could reveal a lot about the group's seriousness toward the implementation of the action plan.

As people volunteered to work on the implementation program, Harper was pleased with his choice. The group displayed the maturity he had felt confident they would. Everyone was concerned about making sure that all the actions were covered. And several in the group were willing to switch from their first choice to their second choice to even out the numbers. One team even volunteered to work on two actions which they perceived as being closely linked.

Each team was asked to devise the steps required to implement their action. That done, they filled out a card for each step detailing the specifics of who, when, where and how the step would be implemented. Much communication took place between teams. In many instances a step required consultation or commitment from someone from another team. Retailers found themselves making decisions usually reserved for head office staff. In the process they discovered a lot about the overall organization that they hadn't been aware of before. The same experience occurred with the head office staff who picked up much about the day-to-day workings of the retail outlets.

The work was fun, the Texaco teams discovered, but it was also serious business. During the session, many teams formed task forces. They scheduled regular meetings to ensure that their action plans would be carried out. Virtually everyone in the room had their personal calendars out on the table. They scheduled meetings, phone calls and other tasks for which they assumed responsibility over the next 90 days. This was no mere exercise. It was a time of making real commitments to real action!

As the teams fininshed their work, they brought up cards that described their steps to the implementation calendar chart at the front of the room. They placed each card in the appropriate week. As the chart began to fill up with cards, excitement grew. Each card contained specific, detailed actions, like "Call John on Wednesday to get budget figures," or "meet with the team on the 18th at 2:00 to decide format and make assignments for the questionnaire on standards criteria." These detailed actions in composite added up to major steps moving the Texaco group in the directions it had mapped out for itself the previous morning. And what had looked so overwhelming the previous evening had quickly and almost effortlessly come together in the morning session.

At the far right hand side of the chart was a column with cards identifying the 90 day goal for each action. As the group examined this column, they saw nothing they felt was unattainable. They were elated at the prospect of the potential achievements for Texaco in just 90 days. Only 72 hours earlier they could not have imagined accomplishing that much in five years!

90 DAY IMPLEMENTATION TIMELINE

Texaco Caribbean Inc.　　　　　　　　　　　　　　　　　　　　　　　　Pine Grove

ACTIONS	DECEMBER	JANUARY	FEBRUARY	90 DAY VICTORY
#2 **Structuring Inter-Organization Communication**		• Assign reps • Sale Contact scheme • Designate office contact • Monthly sales meetings		**Improved Communication**
#3 **Establish Star Recognition Programs**		• Reintroduce Star Award Contest • Develop realistic standards • Facility Survey	• Priority list rehab • Agree on retailer participation	**Improve Company Image**
#7 **Developing Standards Criteria**	• Obtain standards manual • Continuing fortnightly committee meetings	• Establish timetable	• Reproduce and distribute progressively • Reverse poor image	**Standards for 10 Stations**
#9 **Design Appropriate Facility**	• Establish priority system • Conduct field assessment		• Evaluate and agree on final design • Adjust design based on funding	**10 Designs by March 1**
#10 **Develop Q-Q Assurance Program**	• Establish quality check at rack & station • Insure security of tamper-proof seals • Spot check delivery trucks • Establish haulage contractor accountability		• Establish and impose sanctions for Quality & Quantity	**Improved Cash Flow and Involvement**
#12 **Engaging Appropriate Staff**	• Obtain approval to employ • Seek suitable candidate			**Three New Employees**
#13 **Obtain Adequate Financing**	• Establish base volumes • Provide bank/credit statements			**5-10% Increase In Volume**
#15 **Family Orientation Program**		• Retailer orientation tour • Mgmt structure staff organization & functions • Accounting operations procedures	• Appropriation request format • Retailer assessment	**6 Orientation Seminars by 30 March 1986**

As Sherwood Shankland asked the group which steps would have a direct impact on both the head office and for the regional unit, Harper thought, "Every single one of them." But while the group reflected on their experiences and involvement in the *ToP Strategic Planning Session,* which nearly all rated "very helpful," Harper wondered, "Will those plans really be put into action?"

"I think you'll be pleased with the results," Shankland told Harper as they walked out of the room to the team's celebration lunch. That remark, as we shall see, was a major understatement.

Bob Harper and his team called their seminar document "The Texaco Retail Marketing Plan." Subsequent visits to Texaco's headquarters and retail facilities revealed some dramatic results produced by the program.

* * *

Within a year of the *ToP Strategic Planning Session,* Texaco recaptured its former position as the top retailer in the region, overtaking its two major competitors.

The retail stores, having received a major facelift, were bright and attractive. Store operators, once bristling with complaints, now used *ToP Strategic Planning* with their clerks. In fact, the retailers were so sold on the process that they requested a training session for all of their employees.

Bob Harper was completely sold on *ToP Strategic Planning* as well. He saw first hand the results it produced and authorized the ICA to set up the "Texaco Service Training Program" for retail store clerks and operators.

Furthermore, Harper took advantage of the skills of the ICA staff, using them as a sounding board for management ideas. He invited them to work with him for a few weeks on a daily basis to help bring about a new management style and a new system of dealing with the head office.

Harper also extolled the *ToP Strategic Planning Session* to his colleagues in the business community. The process "is an excellent management tool in order for communicating corporate objectives throughout the organization and to obtain a bottom-line commitment toward the achievement of those objectives," he explained.

Texaco's *ToP Strategic Planning Session* involved each of the core methods of **ToP.** These are:

- The *ToP Focused Conversation Method,*
- The *ToP Workshop Method* and
- The *ToP Event Planning and Orchestration Technique.*

Each of these methods is explained in detail in Chapters 4, 5 and 6.

The Texaco *Strategic Planning Session* followed a five-stage process:

- **Mapping Out a Practical Vision,**
- **Analyzing Underlying Contradictions,**
- **Setting Strategic Directions,**
- **Designing the Systematic Actions** and
- **Drawing Up the Implementation Timeline.**

This process will be described in detail in Chapter 7. Other applications of *ToP* methods are described in Chapters 8 and 9.

CHAPTER 4

The *ToP Focused Conversation Method*

Sam, an executive with an international trading firm in Hong Kong, gathered his staff together.

"We have a problem," he explained to them. "We're losing money and it's getting serious. I want to hear what you think we should do about it."

The group considered the problem for a while. But Sam was disappointed. No constructive conclusions nor plan of action resulted from the meeting.

Sam later discussed the meeting with the director of the ICA's Hong Kong office, who asked Sam what sorts of ideas his staff had offered.

"That's why I called you today," Sam complained. "No one said anything. Utter silence. They just sat there most of the time and waited for the next guy to speak up."

It's not surprising that Sam's employees didn't reply to his questions. They probably were afraid they'd lose their jobs if they criticized the way the company was run.

Things might have turned out differently if Sam had posed questions like this:

1. What are some of the most important market indicators today?
2. How has this market activity been affecting us?
3. What do those indicators and their affect on us portend for our future as a company?
4. What are some of our options?

Asking the questions that make the most out of employee wisdom and experience in day-to-day operations is the first of the three basic techniques at the core of the *Technology of Participation*, the *ToP Focused Conversation Method*.

Any number of potential problems are likely to surface in group discussions. They all inhibit progress, retard communication and deter groups from finding solutions. Perhaps a member of the group habitually dominates the meeting or the discussion flounders around aimlessly. Griping may lead to arguments rather than cooperation or the conclusions arrived at are too shallow to be of any benefit. Too often employees leave meetings thinking, "I could really make a difference around here if I could just make myself heard," and feeling disappointed that they rarely are.

Group discussions are better for many purposes than one-to-one conversations. Groups can explore a wide range of questions and can quickly gather data from many people. Groups can bring considerable brainpower together to work out problems and generally save companies much time.

But group discussions must be handled creatively. The remedy for take-charge "discussion hogs" is full participation. The remedy for meandering discussions is a well-planned structure. The remedy for griping is a constructive attitude. And the remedy for superficial conclusions is to dig in and get at the heart of the matter.

The *ToP Focused Conversation* fulfills each of these requirements.

The aim of a *ToP Focused Conversation* is to allow group participants to reflect on an event or commonly shared experience—perhaps a stockholders meeting, a training seminar, a videotape, a news article or book or even a dispute on the production line. *ToP Focused Conversations* help groups interpret such experiences, decide what they mean to the group and draw up appropriate responses.

The value of such reflection is that it helps a group to identify and focus on the true significance of an event. Sometimes important events slip by unnoticed due to a hectic schedule. Other times, a relatively minor occurrence can absorb a group's attention for days because it carries a considerable emotional charge. The *ToP Focused Conversation* helps the group put events into perspective and then respond to them creatively. It also forges a common bond in understanding such events. Only then can the group present a common front in relation to event-related issues. In so doing the *ToP Focused Conversation* provides for meaningful dialogue, results in greater clarity of thought, broadens perspectives and allows everyone to participate.

It takes practice to become skilled at the *ToP Focused Conversation Method*. But managers soon find that with such practice they can lead group discussions that result in clearly stated ideas and well-thought-out conclusions. The method is adaptable to any situation or group, small or large, even to conversations between two individuals.

The *ToP Focused Conversation Method* works because it's a very natural process, based upon the process the human mind goes through when responding to stimuli. This process involves a series of happenings of which we are mostly unconscious. When we reflect on events or experiences, we don't just register the information and file it away in our minds. We analyze it, decide whether to accept or reject it and determine possible uses for it. Through this process, we give meaning to our experiences and determine how to act in response.

The foundation of the *ToP Focused Conversation* is the four steps of the critical thinking process:

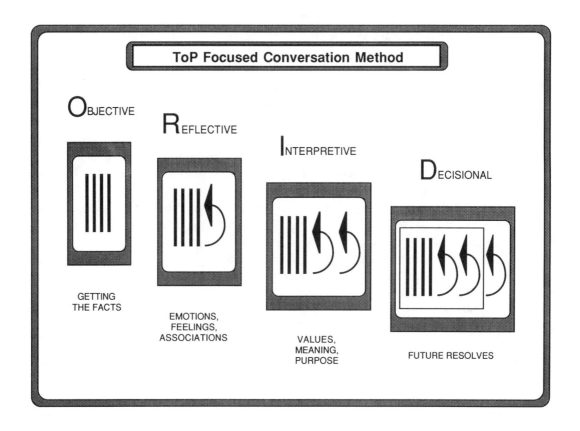

ToP Focused Conversation Method

OBJECTIVE

GETTING
THE FACTS

REFLECTIVE

EMOTIONS,
FEELINGS,
ASSOCIATIONS

INTERPRETIVE

VALUES,
MEANING,
PURPOSE

DECISIONAL

FUTURE RESOLVES

**Objective,
Reflective,
Interpretive,** and
Decisional.

These steps can lead a group from surface observations of a situation to in-depth understanding and response.

The **objective** step draws out the facts about the experience or event. The group recalls information and details that re-create the event so that it's clear in everyone's memory.

How the group feels about the event or experience is the subject of the **reflective** step. Emotional responses and thought associations about the experience are brought into the open and acknowledged.

The third step is **interpretive**. Participants consider the meaning and value of the event and its significance for the group, thereby allowing members to put the event into perspective and determine its impact.

The fourth and final step—**decisional**—is where the group conceives a response by deciding what decision is necessary or what action is required.

To illustrate how natural this process is, imagine you are confronted by a big man carrying a gun.

You quickly note the situation: "He's big, he has a gun, he's asking me for my money and there's nobody else around to help me."

Next you respond emotionally: "I don't want to lose my money, I'm afraid of being hurt or killed, I don't like this man and I want to get out of this situation."

Then you interpret the situation: "I would rather lose my money than my life; this guy wants my money—he'll take it the hard way or the easy way; if I fight, I'm sure to get hurt and probably lose my money too, but if I give him my money he'll probably leave me alone."

Finally, you decide on a course of action. "I will give him my money without resisting. As soon as he's out of sight I'll call the police. And starting tomorrow, I'll never carry more cash than I can afford to lose."

The *ToP Focused Conversation Method* provides a structure that guides groups through those four steps of the natural critical thinking process. Therein lies both the simplicity and the sophistication of the method. It is simple because it follows a natural process—it does not have to be taught. It is sophisticated because it ensures that each step of the natural process is taken, thereby reaching a conclusion based upon the widest base of data possible.

You may wonder, "Why, if this process is so natural, is a structure needed to guide a conversation through it? Wouldn't people follow the process without the guidance?"

In much of our education and training we are taught to short-cut this process and move directly to the interpretive level. We are asked to evaluate and judge things like a poem, a political system, a person's promotional potential or the source of a problem without first gathering all the objective data available. We are also taught that emotional responses are irrelevant or problematic and should be avoided or repressed. Once at the interpretive level, we often stop there, never formulating a response that leads to action.

Beginning at the **objective** level in a group discussion does two things. 1.) It gathers a broad array of data, because people representing different perspectives observe different things in a given situation. The more people and perspectives you have, the more objective data will be brought into the conversation. 2) Beginning at the objective level brings the group to a common ground. They are not asked for their opinions or their judgments but "just the facts, please." This gives everyone in the group a composite, but objective picture of the situation.

At the **reflective** level of a *ToP Focused Conversation,* emotional responses are acknowledged. Emotions are important data. When taken into consideration in making a decision, they strengthen and support the decision. Ignored, they usually jeopardize the decision. For example, a decision to tighten the budget might be made and announced in either of the following two ways. Imagine the outcome of each.

> We are all clear that we will have to make an across-the-board budget cut of 35%. You will all have to go back to your departments and figure out how to keep things running on that basis. We need cooperation, not complaints. I hope this will be temporary.

Or:

Clearly we need to make across-the-board budget cuts of 35%. That's going to be painful for all of us. Some of you are going to be resentful because you think others could absorb more of the cut than your department can. You may even think some are more responsible for our current situation than you are. I would ask that you all turn your eyes to the future. We are all in this together, and it will take all of us to turn this ship around. With cooperation, discipline and team spirit, I think we can be on solid ground in three or four months.

At the **interpretive** level, judgments are made based upon much more data and incorporating a wider range of perspectives than is possible by one person alone or even by a group that has too narrow a focus or ignores pertinent data.

The **decisional** level moves the group to formulate a response and to act on it. This moves the group forward. It helps resolve the situation. Too often, discussions conclude with an opinion but no action. Other times conclusions hang in stalemate because no consensus has been reached. Still other times meetings end in paralysis because no one assumes responsibility for implementing the decision. The decisional level results in action.

Corporations such as Red Lobster Restaurants, Hughes Tool and Pizza Hut, along with not-for-profit and public agencies such the Minnesota Department of Transportation, have found the *ToP Focused Conversation* useful in getting to the heart of situations and issues. The method has forged common frames of reference within diverse groups of people and led to conclusions that have been acted upon.

"The objective, reflective, interpretive and decisional method of questions," Hughes executive J. R. Whanger reported, "is without a doubt a most valuable tool."

Procedure

In *ToP Focused Conversations* one person generally leads, asking questions to which members of the group respond. The conversation leader may also respond to the questions in the capacity of a group member concerned about the issue. The leader should not imply, however, that his or her input is "right," and should not judge answers from group members.

The sequence of questions elicits responses at each level of the critical thinking process. The same sequence of questions is used every time, although the content of the questions varies with the topic.

Step 1. Objective Level

The **Objective** phase of the *ToP Focused Conversation* is a fact-finding mission. By asking each group member to respond, the leader helps them create a shared picture of the "slice of reality" that is the subject of the discussion. The purpose at this stage is to collect basic information. Reflecting on a recent sales seminar, some of the questions might be:

Leader	Responses
What visual images do you remember from the seminar?	The charts of increase in sales rates on the front wall.
	The scene in the videotape where the salesperson closed the deal.
	The intensity in the seminar leader's face when he gave his pep talk
What words or phrases do you recall?	Self-Talk
	Goals
	"He can't buy any less than he's thinking of buying now!"
	The call begins after the prospect says "No."

Step 2. Reflective Level

At the **Reflective** level, the leader asks participants to express their emotional reactions to the event. Questions at that stage might include:

Leader	Responses
What was the high point of the seminar for you?	The personal goal setting exercise.
	The plan for attaining your goals.
	The closing pep talk.
What was the low point?	Analyzing my own sales trends over the past 12 months.
	Watching the sale slip through her fingers in the videotape. It was too familiar.
	Seeing how much effort I've wasted on bad strategies.
What was the collective mood of the group at the end of the seminar?	Inspired
	Motivated
	Challenged
	Confident

Step 3. Interpretive Level

Step three is the **Interpretive** level. These questions zero in on the meaning and impact of the topic, its significance and usefulness to the group. They might include:

Leader	Responses
What would you say was the greatest learning or insight for our group out of this seminar?	The method for analyzing the right market for the product.
	The importance of setting goals, analyzing performance over against goals and reevaluating the goals, not just evaluating the performance.
How would we be different if we acted on that wisdom?	We would do performance reviews every month and reevaluate goals at least once a quarter.
	We would be more sensitive to the market.
	We would be so flexible and responsive we could turn on a dime.

Step 4. Decisional Level

In step four—the **Decisional** level, the questions are designed to help the group identify actions or decisions that may be necessary in response to the experience.

Leader	Responses
What could we do tomorrow to demonstrate that we have internalized the learnings from this seminar?	Frame the sales goals each of us worked on today and hang them outside our doors so they are on public display and we see them each day as we come into our offices.
	Set the dates for monthly sales reviews and quarterly goal reevaluations so we all have them on our calendars.

Here are some examples of conversations that companies have conducted.

On company policy-making:

Objective: What are some of our firm's policies?
What is one policy you've recently been asked to interpret and apply?

51

Reflective:	How do you feel about that policy?
Interpretive:	What is the effect of applying it?
Decisional:	What policies need special attention?
	What kind of special attention do they require?

On evaluating a new business form just put into use in a department:

Objective:	What is the first thing you notice on this form?
	What are some of the key items it includes?
Reflective:	What do you like or dislike about it?
Interpretive:	How does it compare to the previous form?
	How will it make a difference in the way we do business?
Decisional:	What can we do to make sure this form is used properly?

On evaluating a new policy statement from head office:

Objective:	What words or phrases caught your attention as you read this statement?
Reflective:	At what points were you pleased or excited?
	Did anything make you uneasy?
Interpretive:	What implications will this new policy have for our division?
	What changes will be required of us?
Decisional:	What are some of the first steps we need to take to implement those changes?

There are many subjects to which a *ToP Focused Conversation* can bring new insights and meaning. Some of these include:

- having new managerial recruits discuss the elements of effective supervision,
- considering the impact that new government regulations might have on the company's product,
- ferreting out the meaning of a meeting,
- evaluating job descriptions prior to hiring new employees,
- a trends discussion to fit the organization's work in the context of market or international trends,
- interviewing,
- planning a departmental reorganization or
- conducting performance reviews.

Preparation

For best results each *ToP Focused Conversation* should be tailored to the needs of the group. Since the questions must be relevant to the topic and to the group, they should be prepared in advance, using the following three steps.

Step One

Pinpoint the conversation's **rational objective**—what the leader wants the person or group to learn from it. For example, the rational objective of evaluating a management seminar might be to create a consensus of the implications the presentation has for the members of the group.

Step Two

The second step is to target the conversation's **experiential aim**, or what the leader wants the participants to *feel* as a result of the conversation. For the seminar example, the experiential aim might be for the group to sense that the material presented in the seminar was relevant to their situation and that it merits the group's attention.

Step Three

Write out the four-level questions the leader will use to guide the conversation. Writing several questions for each step of the conversation (**objective, reflective, interpretive** and **decisional**), the leader then should review the whole conversation and select the best one or two questions for each step. More than ten questions will make for an unwieldy conversation.

Questions should be specific and open ended. They should not be answered with a simple "yes" or "no." Questions at the objective level should be easy to answer and inviting to help break the ice. As a general rule, there should be two to three questions at the objective level, two at the reflective and interpretive levels, and one or two at the decisional level. This rule is flexible, and with practice, you will learn what works best in different situations.

Tips

Situation	What to do	Examples
Getting Started	• Assure a pleasant climate with no interruptions before the session begins.	"Let's get started. Jim, will you please close the door?"
	• Provide a context as the session begins: what we are doing is important.	"At the annual meeting we decided to establish a more effective communications system. We need to get this in place quickly and smoothly because the whole company is depending on it."

	• First question should be asked with precision. Ask each person to answer the first one or two questions so everyone's voice is heard early in the conversation.	"What are the elements of a good communication system? Jane, why don't we start with you and go around the room to your left."
Keeping track of ideas	• Write brief phrases on your own note pad after each response.	"You mentioned these elements." (Read back the list.) "Which of these is the most critical?"
	• Ask one or two participants to take notes.	
	• Use notes to recap between questions, as needed.	
	• Use notes for writing reports.	
Keeping the discussion going	• If nobody answers, repeat the question. Reword it if necessary.	"OK, someone else, how will a new communications system affect the company?"
	• If participants get off the topic, repeat the question.	
	• If someone grandstands or talks a long time, ask for a specific example. Then ask if someone else has a specific example.	
Maintaining focus	• When the group begins to stray off the subject, recap briefly what has been said so far.	"That is an important concern. Let's bring it up next time we do a problem analysis. Now, will anyone share with us how you think the new communication system will affect the company?"
	• Acknowledge and "bracket" the distraction.	

	• Repeat the question.	
Keeping the discussion practical	• When you introduce the question, give a practical example yourself.	"The video board in the lounge caught my eye the other morning. What are some other practical examples of good communications?"
	• When an answer is abstract or merely gives the person's judgement, ask for an example from their own experience.	
Resolving Disagreements	• You don't have to. It is helpful to have many points of view in the discussion.	"Strong feelings are OK, but we have to get a wide range of ideas, too."
	• If people argue, don't take sides, but ask the group if there are other viewpoints.	"It looks like we have at least three angles to cover. Are there any others?"
	• If someone disagrees, have them say what their own idea is, rather than just disagree.	
Bringing the Discussion to a Close	• Review what was discussed.	"We have covered a lot of ground in a very short while. Now let's move into the workshop to decide on specific action plans."
	• If you made notes, let the group know how the notes will be used.	
	• Tell them when they will receive the results and acknowledge their participation.	

The more you use the *ToP Focused Conversation* Method, the more natural it will feel. You will probably find yourself using it in conversations with your family and friends and applying it more consciously in your own thinking. You will find that your conversations and even your own reflective processes will be clearer, more focused and reach greater depths than before.

CHAPTER 5

The *ToP Workshop Method*

At the core of the *Technology of Participation* is the *ToP Workshop Method*. This method helps a group of people:

- make a decision,
- solve a problem, or
- create a plan.

The *ToP Workshop Method* is particularly appropriate in situations requiring

- innovative and creative solutions,
- multi-disciplined team involvement, and
- urgent commitment to design an action plan.

Like the *ToP Focused Conversation Method,* the *ToP Workshop Method* follows the natural thought process of the human mind as it makes decisions. The method is simple, because it is something we do every day. Yet its flexibility makes it adaptable to innumerable applications and capable of producing highly complex plans. Bringing self-conscious structure to this natural creative process empowers and enriches it.

Although it is based upon the thought process each of us uses several times each day, the real gift of the *ToP Workshop Method* becomes clear when it is applied in a group setting. By tapping and synthesizing the wisdom of people representing diverse perspectives, the method gives rise to decisions and plans that are both innovative and ''do-able''.

Even more exciting is that the process enables the group to reach a consensus quickly. Because everyone in the group participates in building the plan from the bottom up, they all see it as theirs and share ownership of it. Like partners in a start-up venture or parents of a newborn, a sense of partnership is fostered by the activity of co-creation.

The *ToP Workshop Method* consists of five steps:

1. Set the **context**, defining the intent and parameters of the workshop.
2. **Brainstorm** data and ideas.
3. **Order** the data into categories based on similarity of content.
4. **Name** the categories.
5. **Evaluate** the work and its implications.

To illustrate how natural the process is, let's look at a process most of us do each week if not every day—planning your week.

It's Monday morning. You have arrived at your office, greeted your colleagues and poured yourself a cup of coffee. You sit down at your desk and try to figure out how to get started. You pick up a pencil and start jotting down all the things that come into your mind that you have to do this week. You find yourself listing some things that are personal items, like "pick up milk on the way home." You decide that personal items are another list, for another exercise. You scratch the milk off the current list. Then you find some items that are really someone else's job, like mailing a project report to the Hong Kong office. You begin to scratch them off the list. But then you realize that if you don't remind Pat to mail the report, it might not get done. So you decide that this list is not just "things I have to do," but rather "things I am responsible for." By defining the parameters of the list, you are setting the **context** for your workshop.

Now that the context is clear, the list grows quickly. You get out big projects and little things that are easy to forget, but which must be done. This is **brainstorming**. You continue the list until you can't think of anything else that has to get done. You probably have at least twenty items on the list, perhaps many more. To illustrate the process, here is an abbreviated sample list:

> Call Tom for sales figures
> Cancel lunch with Judy on Thursday
> Finance report
> Respond to inquiry from WST
> Remind Pat to mail report to Hong Kong
> Performance review with Kelley
>   "   "   "   Stan
> Meet with BJR re finance report
> Call Roberts to commission survey
> Draft SNT proposal
> Request info on DB software

Next you begin to **order** your list. You put a "P" by all the phone calls, an "L" by all the letters you have to send, an "M" by all the meetings you have scheduled or need to schedule. Several items are major projects that will require substantial blocks of time. You might mark these with a star. You may have many more categories, depending on the type of work you do and the screen you use for ordering your activities. Your list begins to look like this:

P	Call Tom for sales figures
P	Cancel lunch with Judy on Thursday
*	Finance report
L	Respond to inquiry from WST
P	Remind Pat to mail report to Hong Kong
M	Performance review with Kelley
M	" " " Stan
M	Meet with BJR re finance report
P	Call Roberts to commission survey
*	Draft SNT proposal
L	Request info on DB software

You then give each group of activities a **name** and make separate lists for each category. You might make a list called "phone calls" and post it by the telephone. Another list might be called "letters," a third "meetings" and another "projects."

Phone Calls	Letters
Tom re sales figures	Respond to WST inquiry
Judy—cancel lunch Thursday	Request info on DB software
Roberts re survey	
Pat re Hong Kong report	

Meetings	Projects
Performance Review w/ Kelley	Finance Report
" " " Stan	Draft SNT proposal
BJR re finance report	

Now that you have your work ordered into similar activities, you can **evaluate** these activities as appropriate. In this example, evaluating might mean scheduling them according to priority. You might find that mornings are the best time to reach people on the telephone, so you schedule an hour each morning for making phone calls. You might include any calls necessary to schedule meetings so that you can reach people before their calendars are filled. You may prefer to clear your schedule of small but nagging items before you tackle your major projects, so you schedule Monday afternoon to get the letters dictated. Now you can schedule your major projects in the four full days you have freed up, uncluttered by other matters. As you schedule the projects, you might find that you do not have enough time in this week to complete them all. In this case, you prioritize them according to urgency, and find that one or two of them can wait until next week. You can start another list called "Next Week," which will be the beginning of next Monday morning's workshop. This is not irresponsible. It is creative procrastination. It helps "bracket" less urgent work so that you can focus your attention on the work that must get done this week. The finished product, your schedule for the week, might look like this:

TIME	MONDAY	TUESDAY	WEDNESDAY	THURSDAY	FRIDAY
A M	Phone calls ——————————————————————————————→				
P M	Letters	Finance Report		SNT Proposal	

This is just one example of the way most people plan and make decisions all the time. You probably go through this process in varying degrees of complexity several times each day, in planning a project, preparing a shopping list, or thinking through a presentation or report.

The *ToP Workshop Method* brings structure to these steps and ensures that each step is completed before moving to the next one. This is especially important when working with a group because it harnesses the diverse creativity of the members and channels it into one common plan. This is not to say that the various forms of creativity present in the group are limited or restrained. In fact, group members are empowered by the process and by interaction with each other as they focus on the common issue.

Benefits

The *ToP Workshop Method* produces three important benefits when used with a group. These are fresh *creativity*, essential *realism* and committed *implementation*. Imagine, for example, a group representing the design, production, finance, marketing and sales departments of a company coming together for a workshop on product modification in response to customer feedback:

Creativity is sparked by the rubbing together of many ideas from diverse perspectives. The blend of rational and intuitive thinking in the *ToP Workshop Method* fans the flames of creativity to yield a well-conceived product modification plan.

Realism is assured as the limitations of each perspective keep the flames from getting out of hand. For instance, the representative from finance would ensure that budget considerations were reflected in the product modification plan, while the

60

marketing member would prevent budget matters from extinguishing the fire of creativity.

Implementation of the plan is virtually assured because of the commitment shared by those who created it. Just as bran is an important by-product of milling flour, commitment is an invaluable by-product of the corporate planning that takes place in a group workshop. Although the intent of the process is to create an imaginative and workable plan, the commitment of the participants to the plan virtually assures its implementation.

Although the ***ToP Workshop Method*** can be used for almost any kind of planning or decision-making, its benefits make it ideal in situations that call for creative solutions and innovative planning.

Procedure

The five steps of the workshop procedure, once again, are:

1. Set the **context**.
2. **Brainstorm** data and ideas.
3. **Order** the data.
4. **Name** the categories.
5. **Evaluate** the work and its implications.

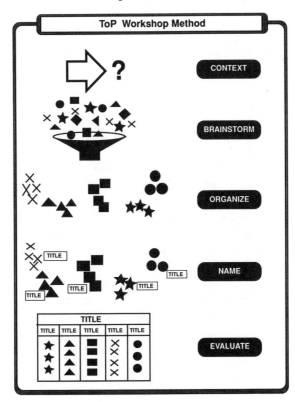

Step 1: Context

To set the **context,** the leader defines the purpose of the workshop, the intended result or product and describes the process and time frame of the workshop.

In defining the purpose of the workshop, the leader states the issue or problem to be solved. This can be done through a statement (the shorter the better), a conversation that allows the group to get involved in the issue or a videotape or study that provides them with background information on the subject. For major planning sessions, a "focus question" is often formulated ahead of time by the *ToP* workshop facilitators in consultation with representatives of the organization or department with which the workshop is being conducted. Examples of focus questions from case studies in this book include:

- "How can we regain our position as number one in market share?"
- "How can we strengthen our unity and develop the leadership capacity to resist infiltration from political factions?"
- "How can we increase production to full capacity?"

By naming the intended product, the leader shares responsibility for completion with the group. Knowing there is a decision to be made or a plan to be completed keeps the group moving forward, rather than getting sidetracked in time-consuming arguments or peripheral discussions.

Describing the process and timeframe of the workshop enables participants to "see where they are going." Knowing that the leader has a plan allows the group to follow the plan, rather than each member trying to solve the issue his or her own way. Knowing the time frame allows participants to schedule other business and errands during breaks or after completion of the workshop. This leaves their attention clear to focus on the workshop subject.

To illustrate the process, imagine a workshop to provide input to the marketing department of an automobile manufacturing company to assist in developing a marketing campaign for a new car model.

The **context** for our sample workshop might go like this:

This car is our major new product for next year, so it is important to our whole marketing strategy. We've brought together people from the design, engineering, marketing, and sales divisions to think through some images and themes that the marketing department can develop into a marketing campaign. We will work together until noon, by which time we will have chosen three images or themes for the marketing department to develop. By this time next week they will share their work with the top executives for final selection of a campaign theme and budget allocations.

Step 2: Brainstorm

The purpose of the **brainstorm** step is to elicit from the group as much objective data as possible. The greater number of people you have representing different perspectives, the more data you will collect. Roger von Oech and other creativity theorists would love this part. By bringing multiple perspectives to bear on an issue, the issue is cast in many different lights, revealing dimensions that had been previously unrecognized. It is something like looking at a hologram. At the same time, each member of the group gains new insights about the issue by seeing it through the eyes of each of the other members of the group. This broadens and deepens everyone's understanding of the issue.

The **brainstorm** process is simple. The leader asks a series of questions to elicit data and insights from the group. The steps are as follows:

1. The leader poses a question and asks everyone to write several answers on paper, then select their best answer.

2. Then the leader asks each person in turn to read aloud their best answer. The leader writes this on a chalkboard at the front of the room so that everyone can see all the data as it comes out (another technique, using 4x6'' cards to collect and display data is described later in this chapter).

3. After each person has given their best answer, the leader asks for additional input. At this point, participants can add to the group's list any items from their own list that are not already on the board.

The **brainstorm** step in our sample workshop might go like this:

Leader's Questions	Responses
What are some attributes of this new car that will appeal to the car buyer?	-High mileage per gallon -Attractive styling -quietness -engineering quality -value (high quality at a reasonable price) -roomy interior and trunk without a "big car" feel -high tech dashboard features -American-made, easy to find parts
Describe someone who you think would buy this car	-Young two-income families -Yuppies -Commuters -Salespeople who are on the road a lot -Young-thinking older people
What are some categories of activity and interest for these people? What do they like to do?	-Running and exercising -computer hacking -making money -dieting -playing golf -outdoor activities

Who are some heroes for this market?	-Ronald Reagan -Oliver North -Crocodile Dundee -Barbara Walters -Indiana Jones
What qualities or values does this market cherish?	-high quality -sophistication -independence -excitement -forward-thinking,-moving and looking -comfort -performance -reliability -assertiveness -fun-loving

Step 3: Order

The process of **ordering** data into similar groupings uses both the rational and the intuitive styles of thinking, with an emphasis on the intuitive. You will notice that those in the group who have greater intuitive prowess will be more vocal in this stage of the process. This is a very creative process because people are naming relationships between data or issues that were previously unseen. New meaning is given to the data in this way. This may sound esoteric, but it is a very natural process and not hard to achieve.

Here's how it works:

1. The leader asks people to read over the list of data on the chalkboard. If it is hard to read because of illegible handwriting or because the writing is too small, the leader may read through the list to refresh people's memories as to what was said in the brainstorm session.

2. Starting with the first item on the list, the leader asks, "What other items on the list are similar to this?" As the group responds, naming similar items, the leader marks each related item with a common symbol, such as a circle.

3. Proceeding to the next item on the list, the leader again asks for similar items, marking this second set with another symbol, such as a square.

4. Continuing down the list, the leader marks similar items with common symbols (creativity is summoned up when the number of categories exceeds the number of simple geometric shapes the leader can think of—triangles, stars, checks, X's, spirals, etc., can be used as needed. It's best to avoid letters or numbers because they imply priority.) until all items on the list are marked with a symbol. If there are a few "stragglers," or unmarked items that don't seem to fit with any of the symbols, they should not be lumped together into a miscellaneous

category. The leader asks the group to look again to see if they are similar to any other items. If not, they are noted and will be dealt with after the next step.

The **ordering** of the items in our sample workshop might look like this:

❏ power

* High mileage per gallon

O Attractive styling

\# quietness

❏ engineering quality

* value (high quality at a reasonable price)

\# roomy interior and trunk without a "big car" feel

Δ high tech dashboard features

\# American made, easy to find parts

❏ Young two-income families

O Yuppies

\# Commuters

* Salesmen who are on the road a lot

O Young-thinking older people

❏ Running and exercising

Δ computer hacking

❏ making money

O dieting

playing golf

outdoor activities

O Ronald Reagan

❏ Oliver North

O Crocodile Dundee

❏ Indiana Jones

❏ high quality

O sophistication

O independence

☐   excitement

☐   forward-thinking, -moving and -looking

\#   comfort

☐   performance

*   reliability

☐   assertiveness

○   fun-loving

Step 4: Naming

The fourth step of the *ToP Workshop Method* is to **name** the categories that have been discerned. In this step the group is making a decision. It is deciding the meaning of the information and the relationships between the bits of information. The group is arriving at a consensus about the significance this information has for the group.

To accomplish this step:

1. The leader asks the group to look at all of the items in the first category of data and give a name to that category. Some questions the leader might ask here are:

   • What are all of these items of data about?
   • What do they all have in common?
   • What is the reality they describe?

2. After several names have been suggested, the leader asks which name best describes that category. Questions here might be:

   • Is this name inclusive?
   • Does it describe all of the items in this category?

3. Depending on the size of the group and the amount of data, the whole group can name each category in turn, or the participants can be divided into teams, each team naming one category of data.

4. Once each category has been named, the leader asks the group to review all of the category names and asks if they are inclusive in their description or analysis of the situation, or if an important element has omitted. In most cases, the group will see how anything that is brought up can be included in one of the categories already named. "Straggler" items from the ordering step generally can be included in a category once names are assigned to the categories. If a major omission is identified, a small group may be set aside to conduct a "mini workshop" to define and describe the omitted category. If the results of the workshop are to be shared beyond the working group, category titles may be refined for consistency and cohesiveness and an overall title given to the work.

QUALITIES VALUED BY OUR TARGET MARKET FOR THE "X" CAR

(ranked by number of items in each category)

- ❏   Power and Performance
- ◯   Sophisticated Style
- #   Comfort and Convenience
- *   Quality and Value
- Δ   Hi-tech Features

To this point, we have been through the first four steps of the *ToP Workshop Method.* We could stop here, give these qualities to the marketing department and tell them that these qualities are what people are buying, and that the campaign they design should emphasize them. But we can go much further. In the hour and a half remaining before noon, we can turn these values into marketing themes.

In our marketing campaign workshop, the qualities to be communicated have been identified. Now, to build a campaign around these qualities the process of **brainstorming, ordering** and **naming** can be repeated, but beginning with a different question. The next level of our sample workshop might go like this:

Leader's Questions	Responses
BRAINSTORM	
What are some components of an advertising campaign?	Jingle
	Celebrity
	Symbol
	Slogan
	Comparative statistics
	Theme song or tune
	"Slice of life" drama
	Story line
	Images that represent the qualities of the product
ORDER	
How would you sort these into categories?	* Jingle
	# Celebrity
	❏ Symbol
	Δ Slogan
	# Comparative statistics
	* Theme song or tune
	Δ "Slice of life" drama
	Δ Story line
	❏ Images that represent the qualities of the product
	# Endorsements (consumer reports, users, trade journals, etc.)

NAME

What names would you give to these categories?

* Music that stays with you
❑ Visual images
Δ Slice of Life
Credibility factors

In many cases, the first level of work provides the screen or framework for the second level. Now individual teams can operate out of a common framework, but focusing their attention on different dimensions of the issue.

To move the workshop to a team mode, the leader gives the following context:

Now we will divide ourselves into four teams, one for each of these categories of components. Each team will brainstorm, order and name ideas that communicate the qualities we named earlier. The music team will come up with several pieces of music or types of music that convey power, sophistication, quality and hi-tech features. The visual images team will come up with images that do the same. The Slice of Life team will create scenarios, or life experiences with which the audience can identify and which reflect those qualities. The credibility factors group will list all the endorsements we have or can quickly get for this car.

Each team works together for twenty minutes brainstorming, ordering and naming their ideas in their assigned area. The total group then gathers to hear the report of each team's work and to synthesize the data.

MUSIC	VISUAL IMAGE	SLICE OF LIFE	CREDIBILITY FACTORS
O Soft Jazz	+ Tiger	* Overcoming a rival	* Celebrity endorsements
* 2001 Theme	+ Cougar	# Seduction	+ Favorable reviews in automotive & engineering magazines
* Star Wars Theme	+ Panther	* Meeting a challenge	
O Deep Breakfast	O Waterfall	# Recognition for accomplishments	
* Synthesized music	O Hurricane		+ Consumer reports
	O Waves		❑ Number of sales
	+ Fox		❑ Market share
	+ Dolphin		* User testimonials
	# Laser		
	❑ Sailing		
	❑ Squash		
	❑ Skiing		
	❑ Hang gliding		

NAMES

* Futuric
O Relaxed but enlivening

+ Wild animals
O Natural energy forms
❑ Physical action harnessing natural power
Delicate strength

* Winning
# Satisfaction

* Personal endorsements
+ Industry acclaim
❑ Popular appeal

Leader

Having heard the reports from each team, let's regroup into the same four teams and quickly sketch out scenarios or story lines for a television commercial. You don't need to write the script, but try to imagine the theme, the music and the image that will remain in the viewer's imagination. If a slogan comes out, share that with us, too.

Team Scenarios

1. Portrayal of a person who takes risks at work (like buying and selling stocks under heavy pressure or a trial lawyer calling the opponent's bluff or an emergency room doctor making life and death decisions) who then leaves work and goes for an equally risky form of recreation (sky-diving, white-water rafting, speed-boating, etc.). Slogan: "For those who want the excitement to continue."

2. Images of humans harnessing natural forces like hang-gliding, sailing, ballooning—then getting into this car to go home.
Music: Theme from Chariots of Fire.
Slogan: "Ride the wind."

3. Images of things that are both powerful and beautiful (a racing stallion, a leaping panther, a roaring waterfall).
Music: "Thus Spake Zarathustra."
Slogan: "For those who believe that power and beauty can be one."

4. Scenes of the car being driven up a beautiful but rugged mountain road, showing off its performance and style.

Music: Chariots of Fire or something with that tone of lightness, strength and beauty.

Narrator: "Never before has one car been ranked Number 1 by both the leading auto industry journal and the consumer reports. [Car Name] is making history."

Step 5: Evaluation

The evaluation step enables the group to reflect upon the work they have done. At this point they state the significance of that work and its implications for their lives as a group and as individuals. By doing this, the product and the consequences of the workshop become a part of each participant's life. They do not walk away as if it now belongs to someone else to implement. It is part of their life and their future.

The evaluation of the sample workshop might go something like this.

Leader	Responses
It's time to draw this to a close, but before we do, let's take a quick look at what we did this morning.	
What do you remember from this morning? What did we do? What did you see, hear, smell?	We described the market this car will appeal to and their tastes and values.
	We clarified some of the outstanding features of the car.
	We developed marketing campaign themes.
	We whistled tunes.
What moods did you experience during our work this morning?	Excitement Frustration Eagerness Confusion Our group got giddy when we were working on the "slice of life." We were running through old ads and old movies plots.
At what points did you notice the mood shift?	When we broke into teams, we felt like we were really sinking our teeth in. Before that the conversation seemed sort of abstract.

In our team, we started out uncertain, not too sure what we were doing. But then the images came faster and clearer and we became more confident and were comfortable with the results we produced.

Doing that last bit about creating a TV ad was fantastic. We had so many ideas popping from the earlier team work and the reports we heard from other groups that I thought they would never come together, but it seemed like our minds just all were moving in the same direction and it just kind of poured out.

How do you feel now?

Elated.

I'm chomping at the bit to go sell some cars.

Quiet confidence.

What did we do today? What did we accomplish?

We got a gut feeling for this car and its buyers.

I know this car. I love this car. I am this car.

We got all of us knowing what each other knows.

We will have a campaign that will win because we believe in it.

What implications will this work today have for you when you get back to your workstations this afternoon?

I'm going to pull together my sales strategy today, I'm so hot!

Now that I have such a clear picture of the market, I have several design ideas that will appeal to them—small ideas like dashboard design, that can be slipped into production without big shake ups. I'm going to go work on them.

We in marketing have to get straight to work on developing these themes for the executive presentation next week. But we are ten times further down the road right now than we would be if we had started without this workshop.

The Card Technique

A popular variation of the procedure described above for conducting a *ToP Workshop* is the use of cards for collecting and displaying the data generated in the brainstorm step. This technique was illustrated in the Texaco story in Chapter 3.

With the card technique, the five steps of the *ToP Workshop Method* remain the same, i.e.,

1. **Context**,

2. **Brainstorm**,

3. **Order**,

4. **Name**, and

5. **Evaluate**.

Only the mechanism for gathering the brainstorm data and ordering the ideas is modified.

Instead of the workshop leader listing the data on a chalkboard or flipchart, the workshop participants print their ideas in bold pen on large cards—ideally 5" x 8" or bigger. The leader uses tape to stick the cards on the front wall or board.

This procedure has numerous advantages.

- The card technique saves time. Participants can record their data and ideas on the cards simultaneously, rather than waiting for the leader to write out each item on a flipchart or chalkboard.

- The card technique allows the brainstorm data to be ordered and re-ordered easily. The leader simply asks the participants to indicate which cards appear to be reflecting related data or ideas and the leader then actually moves the related cards into their ordered groupings.

- The card technique generally affords clearer viewing of relationships among ideas with data on "movable" cards, rather than in lists. Lists tend to keep the individual items of data physically separated. With cards the leader can actually move the data around and "test" relationships.

- The card technique facilitates the ordering process and thereby often improves the quality of the names given to groups of data.

Individuals write their answers on 5″ x 8″ cards.

Teams select their clearest cards.

Cards are passed to the facilitator.

Cards are ordered on the wall according to similar content.

The materials required for the card technique include:

- cards—plenty of large index cards, custom made cards or "Post-its," ideally at least 5" x 8" in size.
- marker pens—one for each participant with tips wide enough that printing can be seen by everyone in the room.
- masking tape—short lengths rolled into small loops for adhering cards to the wall or a chalkboard.
- a wall—large, bare, and of a texture to which tape will adhere (always check this out in selecting a venue; many a workshop has been foiled by brick, fabric or vinyl-covered walls!).

Workshop leaders might experiment with the card technique. Executed well, it is highly effective with groups of virtually any size.

Tips

Brainstorming

How Much Data? It is important to have a substantial amount of data to ensure a comprehensive analysis of the issue. Fewer than twenty items of data would be difficult to work with, especially in the early stages of the workshop. Therefore, in the brainstorm, if you have only three people in the group, ask three or four questions and request that participants list five answers to each, and then select their best two. After going around the group to get their best answers and then getting out additional items, you should be able to arrive at twenty bits of data, even allowing for overlap.

Capturing the Data. Do not try to short-cut the method by eliminating the chalkboard or cards and asking everyone to take notes on their own paper. Besides the fact that most people don't take detailed notes, having the data in front of the room is an important part of the workshop dynamic. It brings the group's attention to a common objective focus. This allows the group to dialogue with the data, rather than with each other, where subjective attitudes may interfere with objectivity.

Ask participants to frame their responses in concise, three or four-word phrases (adjective, adjective, noun is a helpful rule of thumb). This forces precision and clarity, leading to input that is concrete, rather than abstract.

Sticking to the Method. In a brainstorm, all data is received. Nothing is irrelevant, since the question posed triggered it in at least one participant's mind. Sometimes the most "off the wall" bits of data can be very releasing. It's OK to ask for clarification, but don't ask "What's that got to do with this issue?" The leader should gently but firmly steer the group away from rejecting or ridiculing an answer.

Trust the method and ask the group to trust the method. Don't allow speeches and arguments. This method permits everyone's input, treats all data as equal and allows a decision to be made based on data rather than personalities, opinions or power.

Ordering

Avoid naming the categories or groups during the ordering process. This tends to limit them, excluding data that might later be added. The point is to intuitively recognize relationships, and then name the relationship after seeing all its components. Refer to the categories as "the stars" and "the circles" rather than by the content of the categories at this stage.

If an item doesn't easily fit into any group, don't force it. Categories are redefined each time an item is added. This often expands the definition of a category, allowing some of the "difficult to place" items to be included.

Naming

A rule of thumb in arriving at a consensus is that you never criticize or reject someone's model or articulation of the consensus unless you present a better one. In other words, if someone says "I think the stars are all about 'the good life,'" the leader should not accept responses such as, "No, they're not," or "I disagree." Ask for alternative suggestions, rather than reactions, until the group begins to respond in an affirmative chorus: "That's it!" It is helpful for the facilitator to state this rule at the beginning of the session or as the process moves to the naming stage. Then the facilitator can point out when the rule is being violated, pushing for a creative, rather than a destructive dialogue.

Mastering these simple steps will enable you to facilitate your team, department or organization to:

- make decisions that represent a consensus of the group,
- solve problems quickly using a broad range of perspectives, and
- build plans that get implemented.

The next chapter discusses processes for combining and modifying these methods. Knowing the basic methods and the process for weaving them into patterns that suit any situation makes possible many applications that will be illustrated in Part III.

CHAPTER 6

ToP Event Planning and Orchestration Techniques

The *ToP Focused Conversation Method* and the *ToP Workshop Method* described in Chapters 4 and 5 can be applied in groups to facilitate work on many different tasks. These basic methods can be combined and modified in various ways within the *ToP* methodological framework to address many tasks. Some of the most common uses of *ToP* methods are:

> Strategic Planning
> Action Planning
> Team Building
> Philosophy and Mission Retreats
> Leadership Development
> Broad based consensus building
> Organizational Transformation

Several of these applications will be described in Part III.

In this chapter, the finer points of planning and orchestrating *ToP* events are described. Two sets of orchestration skills are explained:

1. **Program Design Procedures**
2. *S.T.E.P.S.* **for Effective Meetings**

Mastering these skills equips the facilitator to custom design *ToP* events for almost any purpose.

Program Design Procedures

Most applications of *ToP* involve the use of a combination of *Focused Conversations* and *Workshops,* but often add presentations, videotapes or studies relevant to the topic. These **Program Design Procedures** enable the facilitator to determine the appropriate use of *ToP* methods to achieve a specific end. There are two phases to the planning:

1. Orchestrating the Meeting Format
2. Orchestrating the Team Experience

Orchestrating the Meeting Format

STEP 1. Develop the Rational Objective

The first step in designing a meeting format is to determine its **rational objective**, just as we did for focused conversations and decision-making workshops. "What is the objective of the meeting?" the facilitator asks. "What is the result we're looking for, or the decision we want to reach? Is it to update the company's marketing plan, perhaps . . . or to create a new five-year vision?"

STEP 2. Develop the Experiential Aim

Once the rational objective is set, the facilitator focuses on the meeting's **experiential aim**, or what mood or emotional tone will enhance and reinforce the rational objective of the meeting. This could be a mood of enthusiasm or excitement or perhaps just a relaxed "feet on the table" mood for talking things over. Will the meeting be a pep talk to bolster a team's flagging spirit, or will it underscore the seriousness of a situation to which no one's paying much attention; a budgetary belt-tightening, for example, or lax quality controls?

When preparing to conduct planning sessions or other *ToP* events with client organizations, *ToP* facilitators typically conduct a *Design Conference* with organization leaders responsible for the outcome of the event. This is a workshop in which the facilitators and the organization leaders jointly determine the key issue to be addressed by the planning session. This issue is formulated as the *focus question* for the planning session. The *Design Conference* serves two purposes. 1) It acquaints the leadership with the *ToP* methods so they know what to expect during the session. 2) Formulating the *focus question* helps to develop the **rational objective** of the session. In most cases, the **rational objective** of the planning session is to answer the focus question. The **experiential aim** may also be developed at the *design conference,* since it will influence the choice of date and venue for the event. Facilitators conducting in-house events within their own organizations can conduct a *design conference* by bringing together those responsible for the outcome and the implementation of the planning session.

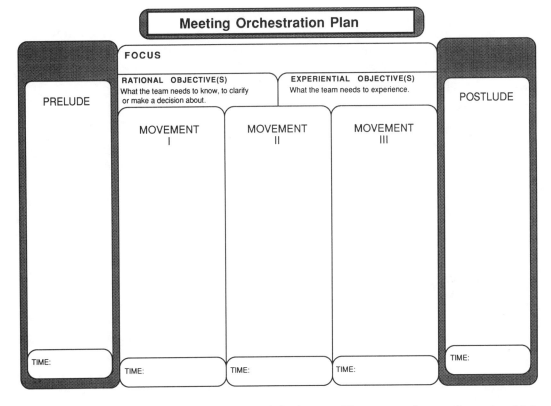

Meeting Orchestration Plan

FOCUS

| RATIONAL OBJECTIVE(S)
What the team needs to know, to clarify
or make a decision about. | EXPERIENTIAL OBJECTIVE(S)
What the team needs to experience. |

PRELUDE

MOVEMENT I

MOVEMENT II

MOVEMENT III

POSTLUDE

TIME:

TIME:

TIME:

TIME:

TIME:

The **rational objective** and **experiential aim** are like camera lenses through which the facilitator adjusts and brings into focus the concerns of the group. Used with precision, they help to ensure worthwhile results.

STEP 3. Orchestrate the Sequential Steps

The final step in orchestrating the meeting format is to plan its "flow" or sequence of steps. An hour-long meeting might start with 10 minutes of conversation or discussion, then 15 minutes of reports followed by a 20 minute workshop, 5 minutes of "checking signals" to make sure everyone understands the intended course of action, and finally, 10 minutes of reflecting on the proceedings.

Planning the flow or orchestration compels the facilitator to think through the dynamics of the entire session. This includes considering which method will be most appropriate, the best way to keep the meeting moving toward its intended goal, materials needed and how much time to allot for each step. A well orchestrated meeting works effectively, whether it lasts only half an hour or two and half days like Texaco's *ToP Strategic Planning Session*. The procedure for planning is the same, but for a longer event, the procedure is followed once for the overall meeting, and then repeated for each module of the program. As if conducting a symphony, the facilitator takes the role of "conductor," arranging the notes (steps) that make up the melody, signaling where the various parts of the orchestra come in and finally, setting the overall tempo of the performance.

Like a musical score, the "meeting orchestration plan" generally opens with a "prelude" or **context** section (a conversation, discussion, or presentation), followed by three "movements" (**brainstorming, organizing** and **naming** in a simple workshop), and a final "coda" or **evaluation**. As we saw in the Texaco story (Chapter 3), this series of steps may be repeated several times to achieve results in more complex tasks.

Orchestrating the Team Experience

An equally important set of considerations involves thinking through the journey of individual participants and the group as a whole. Actually, there are two dimensions here: the **journey toward consensus** and the **journey toward action.**

The facilitator now attempts to identify with the meeting participants' experience, imagining their involvement at each step of the workshop. By empathizing with the participants' point of reference and state of being, the facilitator can fine-tune the questions and the choreography of the meeting.

STEP 1. The Journey Toward Consensus

In the first step, the facilitator thinks through the **journey toward consensus**. This journey follows a path through which the meeting focus progresses from individual participants, to small teams, and finally to the group as a whole. In most sessions, ideas and suggestions are developed individually. Then small teams convene to select items of data for inclusion on the entire group's chart. Next, the group as a whole organizes the data into related clusters. Teams then are assigned one, two or three clusters to refine and name. Finally, the entire group reviews each of the data clusters, decides the order of priority and reaches a consensus on the overall plan.

Keeping the meeting's **rational objective** in mind, the facilitator carefully retraces this individual-to-small team-to-full group progression, and determines if the sequence needs to be modified to fit a particular situation or set of circumstances. For example, the way in which teams are configured can be an important factor, as illustrated in the Texaco story. The facilitator may alter the sequence or team size as the situation requires. The result of this effort is a consensus to which each participant is committed.

STEP 2. Journey Toward Action

The second part of the human journey—the **journey toward action**— describes the process by which the participants develop a sense of urgency and commitment to act on the plans they've forged out during the meeting. The orchestrated flow of context, planning, and reflection provides the motivational spark here, and the facilitator reviews each of these steps carefully to decide how effective they'll be in priming the group for action. Again, the questions or the actual steps might be modified to suit that purpose.

The context step at the beginning of each *ToP* session is a way of focusing the group's attention on the meeting's key issue. The facilitator begins by stating the subject of the session (the focus question) and then identifies the product or result—usually a decision or a plan of action—to be achieved. This can be done in a few short sentences, or the context can be built around a presentation if there is a lot of data the group must absorb.

Sometimes the context can be best established with a *focused conversation* that lets participants go to the core of an issue by expressing their experiences and feelings about it and then reflecting on how it affects their lives and work. Often, two methods are used; i.e., a *focused conversation* and then a presentation. The facilitator decides which combination is best for establishing the urgency of the issue and getting the group inside it.

The facilitator knows that it is during the practical planning stages that the group's creative energy really begins to flow and plans accordingly. Above all, the facilitator wants to make sure that the meeting issue becomes the group's issue. Only then will individual participants give it their all in terms of wise analysis and creative thinking. Such personalized involvement also ensures that each participant is tuned in to the ideas and perspectives of the others.

Finally, the facilitator gives thought to the reflection stage of the meeting. This stage allows individuals, and the group as a whole, to look back on what they've accomplished at the session. This final step gives meaning to the participants' efforts and validates the decisions made or plans adopted as their very own. It bonds the team together and inevitably strengthens their enthusiasm and resolve to get the job done.

This review of the meeting from the perspective of the participants' experience at each step is a fine tuning process. It helps the facilitator refine the questions and the instructions so that they are clear. It enables the facilitator to predict the mood of the group at each stage and to adjust the timing and changes of activity accordingly. Snags can be foreseen and corrected before they occur. This ensures that the group will pursue the most direct path on its **journey toward action**.

Now that the symphony is composed, the facilitator can turn attention to the staging.

S.T.E.P.S. for *ToP* Events

The acronym *S.T.E.P.S.* represents five key aspects of planning for and orchestrating *ToP* events. Briefly, these elements are:

SPACE: Careful selection of appropriate space is important for setting the mood of the meeting and influencing the group dynamics constructively.
Considerations include: location and room selection, seating arrangements, decor, etc.

TIME: Prudent scheduling and disciplined time management establish the tone and importance of the session.
This encompasses date(s), schedule, pace, adherence to agenda time frames, etc.

EVENTFULNESS: Sensitive attention to the human dimension of group interaction leads to heightened enthusiasm and commitment within the group.

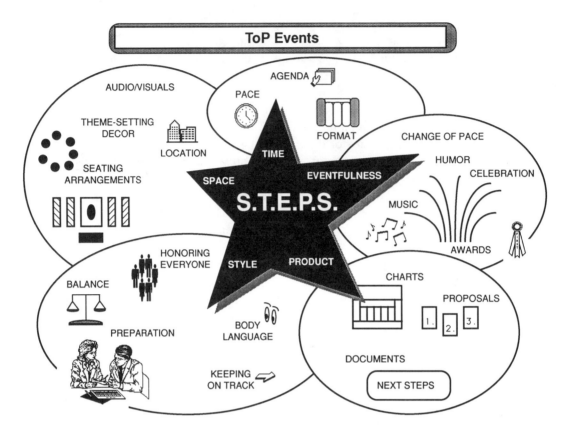

ToP Events

Examples are ice-breakers, change-of-pace activities, humor, celebration, use of symbols, etc.

PRODUCT: Serious attention to producing a tangible product strengthens the group's sense of accomplishment and commitment to action.
This can include decisions, plans, documents, charts, etc.

STYLE: The facilitator's image, role and way of relating to the group and the group process can affect the overall product.

These elements, including the plans and decisions the facilitator must make before conducting *ToP* events, are described in more detail below.

Space

Selecting the appropriate location and atmosphere for a group session is a critical factor in planning a meeting. The space will influence:

- the group's sense of the seriousness of the task and of their importance to it,
- the comfort and effectiveness of the group throughout the process and
- the flow of the process, given the interactive nature of the ToP procedures.

The effective, or ineffective, use of space at a meeting locale can exert a subtle yet powerful influence on the mood of participants and the ability of the group to focus its attention on the issues.

Often when time is short, space considerations are the first to be discarded. Inexperienced leaders tend to view space as a secondary factor. In reality, space is of primary importance, since it dramatically sets the stage for the meeting and announces to the group that: "We're going to do something important here."

By using space effectively, a facilitator can make a group feel special about its mission. No one can force people to be motivated, but the facilitator can create an environment in which motivation is likely to happen —a setting where anticipation, enthusiasm and commitment are more likely to flourish.

Thoughtfully arranged surroundings help people concentrate better, even if they're not totally conscious of those surroundings. And people who concentrate well produce better ideas faster.

Location: The first space criterion is in the selection of the meeting site. If the idea is to get the staff away from the daily hassles to consider broader issues, such as long-range planning or defining the corporate culture and mission, it's often best to hold the meeting at a facility such as a hotel or retreat center. If the goal is to build team spirit, however, it might be better to conduct the meeting in the office environment to demonstrate that camaraderie can happen in day-to-day situations. A middle-ground option is to hold the meeting in a conference room to avoid phone calls and drop-in interruptions but maintaining access to needed files and materials.

Seating: The arrangement of the tables and chairs is another important consideration. Setting chairs around a boardroom sort of table implies formal discussions and decision making. A round table, or comfortable arrangement of chairs in a circle without a table, indicates a less formal event. Tables with participants facing each other and a chalkboard up front signifies that it's a seminar, study or review period, while several small tables for teams sets the stage for a practical "roll up the sleeves" type of session.

Keep in mind that ideas and insights spring from the group, not from the facilitator at the front of the room. For this reason, we encourage seating arrangements that let people see each other's faces rather than the backs of their heads. This acknowledges the fact that the dialogue is between members of the group—not with the "expert" up front.

You may recall that in Hughes Tool's experience, manager J.R. Whanger noted, "In all worker meetings a grouping around a table was used. People sitting around the table facing the middle gave the image of a focus on the real situation in the center. Several times we put a hat on the table to denote a common mind."

The seating arrangement should also include care for the group's needs and comfort. If smoking is acceptable, the facilitator should test the air flow, and put smokers on one side of the room and non-smokers on the other. Paper and writing materials should also be distributed to each table.

Decor and Audio/visual Aids: Meeting room decor and visual aids influence both the group's mood and the focus of attention. Wall space can be used effectively, for example. Facilitators often replace paintings with quotes and symbols that refer to key elements of the process or that describe the principles involved in the planning techniques.

By the end of a ***ToP Strategic Planning Session,*** the front walls are covered with large charts highlighting the vision, contradictions, strategic directions, and 90-day implementation calendar. These remind the participants that they created the plan themselves, building it brick by brick until they had fashioned a house of their consensus. A chalkboard, whiteboard or flip chart at the front of the room also directs each person's attention to the group's common input of data and away from their individual, and perhaps too selective, note pad jottings.

Even if the event is an office party, taking down the usual decor and replacing it with symbols or trimmings appropriate to the occasion demonstrates that "we're in charge of our own environment, our own mood and our own style . . . they don't have to be dictated by our situation."

The space should be clean and uncluttered. This means getting rid of stray papers and dirty ashtrays or removing distracting or unnecessary furniture and decor. A messy or cluttered meeting space makes participants feel that they and the task before them are unimportant. A clean and well cared for environment results in a more receptive frame of mind and stronger motivation to get the job done.

Time

A skilled facilitator makes good use of time, another key factor that influences both the input and the outcome of a meeting.

Dates: The selection of an appropriate date for a facilitated event involves several considerations. These include:

- the urgency of the topic,
- the availability of the participants,
- the requirements for pre-work to be accomplished by the participants before the session,
- the relationship of the required results or session output to other tasks or decisions in the organization,
- conflicting commitments and
- availability of appropriate space.

The timing of a meeting influences the group's mood and establishes the tone and significance of the meeting. Scheduling a strategic planning session on a weekend, for example, implies that the event is important enough for employees to sacrifice their personal time for the sake of the company. Scheduling it on two or three weekdays says the session is important enough to sacrifice employees' productive work time for future results. Both messages are powerful and either one can be appropriate; the facilitator and the manager responsible for the meeting jointly decide which message to communicate and the tone to establish.

Scheduling: In planning a *ToP* event the facilitator develops an appropriate schedule for the steps of the process. The schedule must reflect careful consideration of:

- appropriate start and finish times,
- the familiarity of the participants with the topic and the process,
- realistic time allotments for working through each step in the event design and
- an appropriate pace

During the session, the facilitator should recognize the importance of keeping to the schedule but modify the pace as needed to keep the group moving forward. Knowing how much time to allot for each step helps prevent group frustration at not having enough time to do an adequate job or boredom if the time allotted is more than required for the assigned task.

In a *ToP Focused Conversation,* for example, the **Objective** and **Reflective** level questions are usually answered fairly quickly. If a period of silence occurs, it usually means the group has poured out all the answers they're likely to contribute, and it's time to move on to the next question. At the **Interpretive and Decisional** levels, however, answers tend to take longer and silence is more common between responses. Pushing on too quickly here would make people resent not having a chance to contribute.

Learning to properly pace *ToP Focused Conversations* and *Workshops* takes practice. For the facilitator, like the conductor, timing is critical.

Promptness in beginning and concluding meetings signifies not only that the meeting is important, but that the leader respects the value of the participants' time. Sometimes the facilitator has a tough choice to make. Delaying the start of a meeting until everyone arrives communicates that each member's presence is paramount. On the other hand, starting the meeting on schedule when several haven't yet arrived honors those who made it on time. Either message can be valid, depending on circumstances. A regular weekly meeting, for example, should start on schedule to establish a pattern. Regular attendees will know that the meeting will start with or without them. If the meetings are important to them, they will find a way to get there on time. A special meeting, on the other hand, requiring input from certain people might well be delayed until vital participants show up.

Ending a session on schedule honors participants, recognizing that they have other worthwhile things to do. On the other hand, asking them to remain beyond the announced closing time to finish the work can also communicate the importance of the task. Once again, the facilitator must decide which message to get across. If it's important that the group stay later, the request should be phrased in a way that demonstrates respect for the group's time. A good facilitator will remind them of the value of their work, reaffirm that they have been entrusted with completing a very important task, and will ask them to please put it ahead of their other commitments. Chances are that by that point the group's commitment to seeing the job through is so strong that they will enthusiastically stay to get it done.

The facilitator is also well aware of the group's endurance limits. Sitting for hours on end produces physical and mental fatigue. The average adult attention span is about 18–20 minutes, so it's a good idea to relieve long sessions by scheduling occasional coffee and stretch breaks. These breaks also allow people to make phone calls or handle important errands that might otherwise distract their attention. Someone whose wife is due to deliver a baby or who wants news of an important business deal will have problems focusing on the meeting if not given a chance to check up on those situations.

Varying the pace and type of activity at a meeting is another way to keep the group fresh and energetic. For example, organizing active team discussions right after a long presentation provides a welcome change of pace.

Eventfulness

People respond to spirit-building dimensions of group interaction. Terrence Deal and Allan Kennedy, in their book *Corporate Cultures,* stress the importance of "hoopla" in enriching the culture of an organization.

Meetings sparked with humorous stories, celebrations of individual or corporate milestones, brief relaxation or energizing exercises or special refreshments at strategic intervals are eventful and enlivening. Such eventfulness can be effective in:

- dissolving mounting tension,
- making a transition from one phase of the meeting to another,
- celebrating the group's progress or output, or
- establishing team camaraderie

At one meeting participants found small gifts at their places. The gifts, along with the promise of door prizes to be handed out afterward, helped defuse a stressful session. Such gestures can enliven gatherings, trigger spontaneity, build trust, lift spirits and contribute to team bonding.

Teams can also build identity and pride by creating a motto, slogan, or symbol, or by designing bulletin boards, newsletters, a flag, even pins and buttons. As a continuing feature of corporate life, hoopla has included singing telegrams delivered to employees on their birthdays and humorous skits about the high and low points of the year.

One team at a client organization practices the ritual of weekly debriefings on Friday afternoons to review and poke fun at the week's highlights over beer or punch and chips. A team member reported that the gatherings allow him to put the week to rest and "really enjoy my family over the weekend."

Quarterly evaluations and annual retreats are other great ways to foster team spirit. Last year, a few days before Christmas, the administrator of a large Midwestern medical complex took fifteen managers to a retreat center for the day. It was not what they did that mattered, it was in doing it together that fostered a special *esprit de corps*. At this session, an outside facilitator had the group identify the gifts or unique talents of each team member. The result was an experience of shared trust as each member discovered how the team depended upon him or her.

Tom Malone of North American Tool and Die is an example of a manager who has institutionalized hoopla by celebrating individual accomplishments. He established The North American Tool and Die Freezer Award, a $50 dollar check placed in the plant's refrigerator freezer for any employee who displays remarkable ingenuity. It was named in honor of the first recipient, an employee who discovered that allowing rods to contract in a freezer would enable him to fit an extra part onto the rod ends. Malone also holds Super Person ceremonies and gives awards to those who contribute to meeting the company's goal of zero defects.

Eventfulness takes energy and creativity, but it's worth the effort. Applied with care, it can make meetings and corporate life both more fun and more meaningful.

Product

The most effective meetings result in a meaningful, and ideally, tangible product. Examples of products or "deliverables" might include:

- a written statement describing decisions or directives resulting from the group's deliberations,
- a report or document capturing the group's data, reflections, and conclusions (eg, following a *ToP Focused Conversation*),
- a report or document capturing the group's brainstorming, ordering, naming and action plan (eg. following a *ToP Workshop*)
- a chart or picture of the group's insights and consensus.

Such a product or "deliverable" should be well thought out and in a form that captures the significance of the session without creating a make-work exercise. A product that documents the decision or plan arrived at by the group reminds members of the group's consensus and serves as a guide for future action and progress evaluations.

If a group is allowed to walk away from a meeting hoping that "someone" took good notes and assuming that "someone" will let them know what tasks they're responsible for, they've actually left their initiative and momentum on the table. However, when the document of the group's consensus is put in their hands at the end of the session, the responsibility for implementing that consensus is placed squarely on each members' shoulders. Furthermore, the "event" of receiving a document inspires a feeling of achievement and ownership.

A good technique for building in the creation of a document is to prepare forms for group members to fill out as the session progresses. These forms can then be photocopied and passed out before the meeting closes.

The content and shape of the final product obviously varies in different types of sessions. If the group has worked out a complex plan, the document might be several pages long, and packaging it in a professional looking cover or binder dramatizes its importance.

If the product is a decision, it's helpful to have the group work out the wording, timing, and setting for the announcement of that decision. Details are then typed up and copies distributed to each participant, signifying his or her responsibility for acting on the decision—and accepting the consequences of it.

Style

Facilitation is both a science and an art—a blend of well-practiced skill and sensitive attention to people. The facilitator displays the finesse and presence of an orchestra conductor who inspires musicians to peak individual and symphonic performance.

ToP facilitators master *ToP* techniques and employ a style which fosters group creativity and commitment.

Technique and style are complimentary, not synonymous. Great style in the absence of technique or method seldom yields productive results. Solid technique or sophisticated methods can prove dry and even counterproductive in the hands of an authoritarian or lifeless group leader. Effective facilitators work to master both the techniques and the style of their craft.

Important elements of facilitator style include:

- relaxed alertness,
- realistic optimism,
- assuming responsibility for the task, the process, the outcome and the participants,
- genuine care for the welfare of the group and the organization,
- honoring the wisdom and creative potential of the group and each individual participant,
- flexibility and responsiveness while keeping the group on track,
- encouraging participation while discouraging individual dominance or sidetracking,
- providing objectivity,
- buffering criticism, anger and frustration to enable the group to progress.

Specific techniques can be applied by facilitators using **ToP** to manage successful meetings.

For example, the facilitator is an evocateur. The role and style is not to instruct but to elicit ideas and answers from the real experts—the members of the group.

To do this, *ToP* facilitators use question after question to bring forth the insights of the participants, clarify those insights and help the group forge them into a consensus to which everyone is committed. The questions are phrased so that they can't be answered with a simple "yes" or "no." Instead of the question: "Can we change that?" the facilitator asks "*How* can we change that?" Such open-ended questions keep the ideas flowing, whereas a "yes" or "no" answer often stops the flow of the conversation.

Assuming that every participant has important perspectives to contribute, the facilitator draws out naturally quiet people, even if that requires having naturally dominant personalities listen more than they are accustomed to doing. This is often done by going around the room, asking each person in turn to answer the first question or two out loud. That gets everyone involved from the very beginning. The entire group then knows that everyone's contribution is both expected and respected.

One of the facilitator's most important roles is to help the group achieve objectivity. One way to do this is to grant equal recognition to every idea put forth by any member of the group. The facilitator refrains from criticizing or judging any participant's comments and discourages other participants from doing so. The facilitator may ask a question to clarify an unclear idea or indicate when a response is out of step with the procedure. A response offering a **strategic direction** when the group is in the **underlying contradictions** stage, for example, will be redirected in a non-critical style, such as, "You're a little ahead of the game. We'll get to that as soon as we name the contradictions." The facilitator affirms the participation of every individual, yet maintains objectivity by not advocating any particular idea.

Another technique to maintain objectivity is to keep the group's attention focused on the data rather than on each other. This keeps personalities and personal differences from dominating the session. The facilitator does this by putting the answers up on a board at the front of the room so that everyone's attention is directed there, instead of at the person across the table.

In most workshops group members write out their answers on cards, then pass them to the facilitator who tapes them on a chalkboard or chart. Besides saving the time it would take for the facilitator to write out each answer on a blackboard, this guarantees anonymity for the author of each idea. It enables timid people to express their thoughts and ensures that all ideas will be heard, regardless of who proposed them.

When a participant offers a statement of what he or she believes reflects the group's consensus, no one is allowed to criticize that statement unless they come up with an alternative. Simply saying "That's wrong" or "I don't agree" is destructive to the process. In such instances the facilitator asks the dissenter to offer a better statement, phrased in a way that expresses his or her own insights without negating the original idea.

Using these techniques, facilitators can share their confidence in the *ToP* methods with the group which learns, through objective experience, to trust the methods as well. Over thirty years of experience with *ToP* methods has shown that *ToP* encourages participation, allows information and insights to be offered for serious consideration, and permits decisions to be based on objective data rather than on personalities, power or eloquence.

The confidence level and professional image projected by facilitators can be enhanced by the following disciplines:

- Study and practice the *ToP* methods and participative techniques.
- Do appropriate homework to gain knowledge of the organization's history, culture and objectives.
- Consult with key representatives to pinpoint issues prior to planning a meeting.
- Prepare a thoroughly orchestrated plan for the session which accounts for the group attending and the product desired.

Using such disciplines, the skilled facilitator makes each session hum with creative energy, enabling team members to make intuitive leaps and develop clear images. These fresh, insightful images will lead to solid decisions, plans and commitment to action.

The techniques and style of *ToP* facilitation are valuable for leaders of teams or departments within organizations, as well as for those working as consultants for other organizations.

Gerry Tessman, director of the Department of Employee and Organization Development at the Minnesota Department of Transportation, said that many of the Department's staff were trained in the methods of *ToP* facilitation. He reported that "they were able to integrate them into their departments and adapt the methods to suit their organization. They found these methods for leading meetings to be tremendously effective."

In particular Tessman noted, the Department discovered that "if you have a structured agenda and stated purpose to accomplish, you don't have all the diversions and slowness. So they found that a meeting facilitated with *ToP* methods is much more productive. It helped them make terrific progress and totally changed the way they do meetings."

The Minnesota Department of Transportation found training their people in *ToP* methods was a major factor in the agency's 90% accomplishment rate of its proposals.

We have now explored the Program Design Procedures and the five elements of *S.T.E.P.S.* that comprise the *ToP Event Planning and Orchestration Technique.*

In Part III we will take a closer look at how these basic techniques can be combined in various ways in a wide range of applications.

PART THREE

Applications of the *Technology of Participation*

CHAPTER 7

The *ToP Strategic Planning Process*

The methods of the ***Technology of Participation (ToP)*** described in Part II are highly effectives in a wide variety of situations. They can be used as "stand alone" tools, which any manager would do well to carry at his or her side for problem solving, leading discussions and orchestrating meetings and other events. The most dramatic demonstration of their power, however, is when they are woven together into a seminar or program that enables an organization to accomplish major planning tasks.

ToP methods have been applied to accomplish a wide range of tasks. These have included time management, customer service, leadership training, mission and philosophy retreats, team building and organizational development and transformation. In the following chapters we will describe several applications of ***ToP*** that have been developed and tested with a wide variety of organizations. These include:

Chapter 7 ***ToP Strategic Planning***
Chapter 8 ***ToP Leadership Development***
Chapter 9 ***ToP Philosophy and Mission Retreat***

Program applications of the highly flexible ***ToP*** are tailored to meet the specific needs of particular organizations. Therefore, there is no such thing as a "canned" program. These chapters will, therefore, describe some of the most common elements and formats of these programs, while underscoring that there are always variations.

The ***ToP Strategic Planning Process*** is one of the most popular ***ToP*** applications. It has been the introduction to ***ToP*** for many organizations looking for a process or a facilitator to help in strategic planning. Many of these companies discovered that employing participative techniques could benefit many other aspects of their organizations.

The story of Texaco Jamaica, told in Chapter 3, illustrates the ***ToP Strategic Planning Process***. The process was originally developed in the early seventies and has been used with corporations, local communities, government agencies and organizations of all types across the world. It has been called by many names, including *LENS* (Leadership Effectiveness and New Strategies), *Human Development Consultations,* and *Strategic Planning and Implementation.* Most of the other applications of *ToP* were developed in response to organizations that had benefitted from the *ToP Strategic Planning Process* requesting that the same techniques be applied to other specific issues or concerns within their organizations.

To understand why the *ToP Strategic Planning* is so effective, it might help to examine some recent observations about strategic planning by management experts.

> According to a survey reported in *Training* magazine, strategic planning is the third most important subject addressed in executive development programs.

> Daniel H. Gray observed in the *Harvard Business Review* that, ''though it seems as if strategic planning is on the way out in some companies . . . , I would say, on the basis of my research and expertise, that reports of its demise are exaggerated and premature. If you do it well, you evolve beyond strategic planning to strategic management.''

> Robert H. Hayes observed that strategic planning is useful if properly applied, but too often it's not. ''Let's face it,'' Hayes wrote, ''Strategic planning, as practiced by most American companies, is not working very well. . . . One or more of three reasons is usually cited:

> 1. most companies do not really engage in planning but simply carry out an annual ritual;
> 2. planning is carried out largely by outside consultants and corporate staff personnel, and therefore is becoming increasingly divorced from the realities of the business; and
> 3. plans, once developed, tend to be too inflexible and constraining in rapidly evolving competitive environments.''

The *ToP Strategic Planning Process* responds to each of Hayes's critiques:

1. *ToP Strategic Planning* follows a process that begins with developing a common vision of the organization's future and ends with the construction of an implementation timeline complete with assignments, deadlines and scheduled review sessions.
2. The *ToP Strategic Planning Process* may be facilitated by outside consultants, but (using the methods described in Part II) the decisions are made by the members of the organization. A wide cross-section of the organization is usually represented, so that decisions are based upon the current realities of the business as experienced by those closest to them.

3. The *ToP Strategic Planning Process* results in plans that are flexible and includes review sessions for updating and revision on a regular basis.

Gray's article concluded that "Companies trapped in half thought-out planning may . . . avoid the front-end costs of participation, discussion, and explicit detailing, but they pay the cost of not seeing their options, not reaching their goals, and spending days bogged down in implementation."

The *ToP Strategic Planning Process* results in a plan that is comprehensive and long ranging, while at the same time so detailed that implementation begins the day the planning process is completed.

Overview of the *Top Strategic Planning Process*

The *ToP Strategic Planning Process* consists of five steps:

1. Mapping Out the **Practical Vision**
2. Analyzing the **Underlying Contradictions**
3. Setting the **Strategic Directions**
4. Designing the **Systematic Actions**
5. Drawing Up the **Implementation Timeline**

While many of these components are common to other strategic planning approaches, *ToP Strategic Planning* is unique in three ways:

1. The flow, or sequence, of the steps
2. The use of the *ToP* methods to involve the group
3. The emphasis on implementation as part of the process

The Sequence of the Steps

The *ToP Strategic Planning Process* begins by having the entire group create a statement of their common, **practical vision** for the organization. This provides a common focus and direction for planning. Unlike some approaches that start by naming the problems facing the organization, *ToP Strategic Planning* assumes that a situation can only be interpreted in the light of a vision.

Thus, the second step in the process is to name the **underlying contradictions.** These are situations, both internal and external, that obstruct the realization of the common vision. This is the point at which *ToP Strategic Planning* differs from goal-oriented approaches. It allows groups to "work smarter" by removing roadblocks, rather than just "working harder" trying to accomplish their vision without a clear focus on what blocks, or contradictions exist.

The third step is setting the **strategic directions**. These are projects, programs, campaigns and agendas that address the underlying contradictions, paving the way for the vision to come into being.

Designing the **systematic actions** is the fourth step. Specific actions are described that will implement the strategic directions. They are prioritized in terms of urgency and importance.

The fifth step, drawing up the **implementation timeline,** consists of the "action detailing." Those systematic actions scheduled for the first quarter implementation are fleshed out in terms of the nitty-gritty details. These details include what steps are required, who will do them, what resources are needed and what the victory will look like. The *ToP Strategic Planning Process* is not finished until this step is done.

These steps will be explained in more detail later in this chapter.

The Use of *ToP* Methods to Involve the Group

The second aspect of the uniqueness and the effectiveness of the *ToP Strategic Planning Process* is the use of the *ToP* methods described in Part II of this book. In most *ToP Strategic Planning* sessions, each step of the process consists of a *focused conversation,* a presentation on the process (such as the role of the **Practical Vision**), and a workshop to gather input and reach a consensus. In many cases, other resources are used. Videotapes, articles or excerpts from a relevant book, sometimes serve as the topic for a *focused conversation* or take the place of a presentation.

The *ToP* methods bring together the insights and experience of a broad spectrum of participants, which brings comprehensiveness and realism to the planning process. They also generate commitment and motivation on the part of those who participate in the process. The more who participate, the more widespread is the commitment to the plan. Some organizations have used the *ToP Strategic Planning Process* to gather input from every department toward the overall strategic plan for the entire organization. These organizations have learned the benefit of group involvement in approaching strategic planning. They share Daniel Gray's view that "It is now widely accepted that strategic planning is a line management function in which staff specialists play a supporting role," and that "good action detailing . . . requires the participation of middle and lower management and the work force." Gray's conclusion is that lower level participation is highly desirable because, "those below know the terrain. . . . Through such participation, managers generate the kind of understanding, ownership, commitment and motivation necessary for successful implementation. The alternative, which is to try to push strategic planning out into the organization and down through the ranks by exhortation and other forms of one-way 'communication,' has only minimal effect."

Speaking from a different perspective, Rae Barrett, general manager of SEPROD, a manufacturing company in Jamaica, describes the role of the *Top Strategic Planning Process* in the decision-making process at his company.

". . . Too often, people confuse participation in the decision-making process with the responsibility of the decision-maker. Decision-makers are held accoountable for their decisions by the organization and this responsibility cannot be delegated to another individual or group of persons. In participative decision-making, we seek to have decision-makers avail themselves of the full range of expertise and experience that is at their disposal in the organization so that the decision-maker can make the most informed decision. Furthermore, studies on motivation have shown repeatedly that when people are exposed to the process by which decisions which affect them are made, they share a sense of participation in the decision and are more responsive to such decisions.''

The Emphasis on Implementation as Part of the Process

A third uniqueness of the *Top Strategic Planning Process* is that it does not stop at the level of strategy, but moves right into implementation. In fact, the last two steps in the five step process lay out the specific actions that will implement the strategic plan.

Although many complex plans remain on the shelf, Gray's survey found that an even more frequent problem is that plans are too general. He reported that ''Approximately seven out of 10 companies in our sample do not carry the formulation of strategy much beyond some general statement of thrust such as market penetration or internal efficiency and some generalized goal such as excellence. Having only generalizations to work with makes implementation very difficult. Targets don't mean much if no one maps out the pathways leading to them.''

Gray concluded that ''the cure for half-baked strategy is action detailing.'' That is exactly the sort of detailing that takes place in the final step of the *ToP Strategic Planning Process.*

Now let's examine each of the five steps of the *ToP Strategic Planning Process* in more detail.

The Steps of the *Top Strategic Planning Process*

The five steps of the *ToP Strategic Planning Process* each address a specific question. These are:

1. **Practical Vision** — What will our organization look like five years from now?

2. **Underlying Contradictions** — What stands in the way of the realization of our vision?

3. **Strategic Directions** — What arenas of activity will resolve the contradiction and release the practical vision to come into being?

4. **Systematic Actions** — What specific actions will implement the Strategic Directions?

5. **Implementation Timeline**   What steps are required to
                                      implement this action? How will
                                      they get done? Where? By whom?
                                      By when?

Depending on the organization's size, structure and needs, the *ToP Strategic Planning Process* can take from six hours to two and one half days. In some sessions, each step includes a presentation, a *focused conversation* (sometimes three) and a *workshop*. Other sessions might emphasize only the *workshops*, sprinkling *focused conversations* in occasionally.

Each *ToP Strategic Planning Session* is carefully tailored to meet the needs of the organization and its staff. This is frequently done through a *Design Conference*, as described in Chapter 6. In some cases, managers of the organization are trained as co-facilitators. In others, special components are added, such as reports from departments, presentations or studies, etc. For the sake of clarity, this chapter will focus on the *workshops* used in each step of the process. This is not to diminish the value of the other methodological components. They can greatly enhance the planning process, lending different texture and dimensions, depending on the need. However, the variations are so numerous, it would take another book to describe all the options and combinations that have been applied.

Mapping Out the Practical Vision

In every instance of a flowering culture there had been a positive image of the future at work.

Fred Polak
Dutch Futurist

One of the hallmarks of a successful organization is that they have vision—they know where they're going.

Larry Wilson
Co-author
The One Minute $ales Person

An effective organization must share a vision or sense of purpose that all its employees can articulate.

John Parr, Director
Center for Public/Private
Sector Cooperation

The leader is not responsible for the vision, but that there be an ongoing process of visioning throughout the organization.

Peter Senge
Innovation Associates

Vision is a concept that is receiving a great deal of attention today. Being a visionary is considered by some to be a prerequisite for leadership. This is true for organizations as well as for individuals.

The *ToP Strategic Planning Process* begins with the articulation of a common *Practical Vision.* This provides the direction toward which an organization can move and align itself. The clearer the vision, the more focused the strategy.

The most powerful, driving, unifying visions share several qualities:

1. They are concrete and specific.
2. They are bold, challenging and exciting.
3. They are attainable.

A good example of the power behind vision lies in John F. Kennedy's inaugural declaration that we would put a man on the moon and return him safely to Earth by the end of the decade. Had he said, "We're going to have a better space program," the remark would have generated little interest. Instead, he created an image with flesh and blood, with specific objectives and timeframe. That one statement galvanized the entire race to the moon, because it provided Americans with a specific, vivid picture of its future in space.

The *Practical Vision Workshop* in *ToP Strategic Planning* elicits from participants the images that form the basis of their common, practical vision. It then helps them forge those images into a vision that is concrete, challenging and attainable.

The *Practical Vision Workshop* begins by asking participants to imagine they are standing five years in the future and describe what they see. The question can be embellished by asking them to imagine that they are taking a visiting reporter/photographer on a tour of the plant, or that they are writing a newspaper article about the changes and accomplishments of the company over the past five years. They are asked to describe specific sights, as if they were taking photographs. This helps them to focus on specific, concrete images.

Following the steps described in Chapter 5, the workshop proceeds, as each individual makes a **brainstorm** list of their own images, then selects the three they consider to be most significant. Then small teams are configured, selecting five to seven images from among all those contributed by each member and writing them on 5″ x 8″ cards. The facilitator reminds the teams to write clear, concise and concrete images on the cards. In response to the facilitator's request for the clearest image, then the most futuric, then the most unique, the teams pass their cards forward to begin composing the mosaic that will become the group's common practical vision.

As the images are put up on the wall or a chart at the front of the room, the group participates in **ordering** them into categories of *similar images.* When all the cards are up, the group reflects upon the categories and the relationships between them. They look for patterns and points of commonality, as well as of diversity, in their vision. They also check for comprehensiveness, noting any gaping holes in the vision, like no mention of the product or service they will be delivering in five years.

Each category is then **named**, defining a key component of the vision. This can be done as a whole group, or in teams, depending upon the size of the group and the timeframe of the session. Teamwork fosters greater participation, but each team only focuses on a piece of the vision. With the whole group naming each category, a few vocal and articulate people can often dominate the session, but everyone participates in naming every category. Each participant is therefore "inside of" the whole vision, rather than just the one category they worked on naming with a team.

Once all the categories are named, the whole picture is once again **reflected** upon and the consensus is stated. Usually, the vision as it emerges in the process is the consensus and the reflection reveals this. Sometimes, however, there are critical points of diversity, and these must be addressed in order to reach a consensus on the vision. This can sometimes be done in the reflection process itself. Otherwise, it may be necessary to set aside a small team to conduct a mini-workshop on points of diversity and bring back a recommendation to the group. Such a team must be comprised of all the various perspectives that are critical to the issue.

A chart of the group's practical vision is drawn up and becomes part of the document distributed to each participant at the end of the session. A wall-sized chart is also drawn up and put at the side of the room, as a reference point for the next session.

Analyzing the Underlying Contradictions

Once the common **practical vision** has been articulated, the **contradictions,** or blocks to the realization of the vision can be identified. The question addressed by this session is, "What obstacles, or roadblocks obstruct the realization of our vision?"

Contradictions are not problems. They are windows that allow the group to see where it needs to move in order to achieve its vision.

Contradictions are positive, not negative. They are existing realities, not absences or vacuums. For example, "Lack of money" is not a contradiction, but a situation. "Poorly prioritized budget" is a contradiction that might be illumined by the practical vision.

The process of analyzing the underlying contradictions does not involve solving isolated problems, but identifying the root causes of many surface issues. Analyzing contradictions is like a doctor diagnosing the cause of an illness in order to cure it, rather than just treating the symptoms; or like weeding dandelions out from their roots, rather than just cutting them down, only to see them growing back within a few days.

The *ToP Workshop* method brings together the diverse experience and wisdom of a group to identify those common, underlying obstacles to their vision.

The **Underlying Contradictions Workshop** begins with the group reviewing the chart of their practical vision. They are asked to individually **brainstorm** on their paper at least one block, or obstacle for every column or category in the vision chart. When they have finished, each participant marks the two or three most critical items on their list.

Again in teams, each member shares his or her starred items. Together, each team selects five to seven obstacles from among all those shared and writes them on cards. They are reminded by the facilitator to write positive, concrete statements, preferably as three-word titles. They are also asked to number their cards consecutively.

The facilitator asks each team to send up its cards numbered 2, 4 and 6. This provides a random selection of blocks from each team. As they are placed on the wall or chart, the facilitator begins to **order** them in clusters according to *common root causes.* If any card is unclear or stated negatively, the facilitator will ask the team that submitted that card to rewrite it. Once several categories have clearly begun to emerge, each is assigned a letter. The facilitator asks the group, "What is the underlying cause of all the blocks in this category?" A one word holding title is given to each group of cards. The facilitator then might ask the groups to look at their remaining cards to see if they find any that do not fit into any of the existing groups. As these cards are passed forward, some may be found to fit into existing groups after all, when other teams see the cards. Or several "misfit" cards may go together to form a new group. A few may be true "stragglers" and stand alone for the moment.

Finally, the facilitator asks the group to mark on their remaining cards the symbol of the group each card goes with and pass them forward. Once all the cards are on the chart, the group reflects upon the groups and the existing patterns of obstacles blocking the realization of their vision. One common observation is that almost every group contains blocks to many different components of the vision. There is no one-to-one relationship between the contradictions and the vision components.

The group reflection informs the process of **naming** of the groups. The naming process is critical, because it interprets a pattern of relationships, names that pattern, thereby objectifying a reality that was hitherto unrecognized. Once again, the groups of data can be named by the whole group or by teams. Either way, however, it is important to allow the whole group to reflect in depth on all the groups and their names at the end, to ensure ownership and consensus by all.

During the **evaluation** at the conclusion of the **Underlying Contradictions Workshop** the group is usually exhausted, sometimes depressed, sometimes relieved and sometimes all three. The exhaustion comes from working hard at being honest with themselves. The depression may come at seeing the number, size and weight of the obstacles, which may have not been seriously considered before. The relief comes from having brought many things to light that were previously hidden, and from seeing them named and therefore objectified—it makes it easier to see how to gain leverage on them.

The chart of **Underlying Contradictions** is prepared, listing each contradiction with all the cards underneath it, in descending order from left to right. It is placed at the side of the room for reference in the next session on **Strategic Directions**. A one-page copy is also prepared for the final document.

Setting the Strategic Directions

The **Strategic Directions** session is a pivotal point in the *ToP Strategic Planning Process*. This is the beginning of the creation of an action plan. The **Practical Vision** and **Underlying Contradictions** workshops employed visionary and analytical thinking. The **Strategic Directions** workshop will call upon strategic thinking.

Strategic Directions are broad directions or proposals that deal with the **Underlying Contradictions**. They may be direct, addressing a contradiction head-on to remove it, or they may be indirect, circumventing the contradiction. They often take the form of new programs, projects, campaigns or systems.

Because they address the contradictions, rather than the vision, strategic directions tend to be broad and comprehensive. There are likely to be as many that focus inward as there are that focus outward.

Creativity and innovation are the keys to setting the **Strategic Directions.** A presentation or conversation highlighting ''bold moves'' is often used at the beginning of this session to provide fresh images of innovative actions and the multiplicity of ways to approach contradictions. The **Strategic Directions Workshop** begins by having each individual review the chart of **Underlying Contradictions**. Then participants list at least two different proposals to deal with each contradiction and mark their three best proposals. Each team then selects five to seven proposals, taking care to balance venturing and conserving proposals, but emphasizing the venturing ones. The selected proposals are written on cards, color-coded according to the contradiction they address (if there are not enough different colors of cards, they can be marked with the symbol of the contradiction they address).

With large groups (20 or more), each team may be assigned to work on two or three of the contradictions. In this case, each individual **brainstorms** at least three proposals to each contradiction and stars one item for each. Each team then selects from among the individuals' contributions six to eight proposals for each of its assigned contradictions, making sure that the set of proposals is balanced and comprehensive enough to resolve the contradiction.

When the teams have finished their work, the facilitator asks each team to pass forward the clearest proposal, the one that needs no explaining. Next, each team is asked to pass forward a proposal that is very different from any of those submitted in the first round. As the cards are passed forward, the facilitator places them on the wall in columns. They are **ordered** in columns according to similar *intent*. If there are more than two columns with only one card, the facilitator might ask each team to send forward one more card. Once the columns hold fairly distinct clusters of data, the group reviews the content of each column and gives each a one-word holding title that captures the essence of the intent of the cards in that column. Then the teams mark each remaining card with the symbol of the column in which it belongs. These cards are passed forward and put on the wall in the columns indicated by the symbol on the card.

When all the cards are placed in columns, the group reflects upon the columns, noting which ones have the most cards, the least cards, the greatest mix of colors of cards (which reveals columns that have converged out of proposals to many different contradictions), and relationships between columns. The facilitator directs the group's attention to the column with the greatest number of cards and asks, ''What is it we intend to do in this arena?'' When the group reaches a consensus on the **name** for that column, the rest of the columns are named, either by the whole group or by teams.

A final reflection, or **evaluation** upon the strategic directions helps the group internalize the directions, observe the balance between bold and conserving directions, and notice their own state of being as they review the decisions they have made about their directions for the coming year.

Designing the Systematic Actions

The cure for half-baked strategy is action detailing.

Daniel H. Gray

Having defined the **Strategic Directions** that will surpass the contradictions, the next step in the *ToP Strategic Planning Process* is to design the specific actions that will "put wheels under" those directions. These are actions that will be implemented within the coming year.

Systematic Actions (or tactics, as they are sometimes called) are specific actions that stand on their own. There are usually several such actions that, together, serve to implement a **Strategic Direction.** For example, a **Strategic Direction** like "Inter-Departmental Communications System" might be implemented by several **Systematic Actions** such as, "Initiate In-House Newsletter," "Electronic Mail Linkage," and "Monthly Department Head Meetings." **Systematic Actions** take more than one person and one day to accomplish, but they are specific, concrete and measurable.

The **Systematic Actions Workshop** begins by dividing up the **Strategic Directions** by teams. Each team is responsible for one to three **Strategic Directions.** In each team, individuals **brainstorm** two or three practical, independent actions that would accomplish each of the **Strategic Directions** for which their team is responsible. Each person marks the most effective action on their list for each direction. The team then gathers each member's starred items for each direction. The team reviews the list, asking whether the actions are practical, attainable and realistic, and whether, if they were all implemented, the **Strategic Direction** would be fulfilled. Duplicates are eliminated and a list of 7–10 actions for each direction is written on cards (one action per card).

The whole group regathers, and each team is asked to send forward two cards that represent the most substantial actions for each of their **Strategic Directions.** These actions will require the most time and the most people to accomplish. The facilitator places these actions on the wall in clusters, **ordered according to** *similar actions.* The facilitator then asks for two more actions per direction—substantial, but different from those already on the wall. These are added to the clusters. As long as unique actions continue to be submitted, the facilitator continues to call for more data. Once the cards all begin to fit into existing clusters, those clusters are given holding titles that define the action arena described by the cards. The teams then mark their remaining cards with the appropriate symbol for the cluster into which they fit and pass them forward.

When all the cards are up in clusters, the group reflects upon what the action arenas reveal. Some important points to note are:

> Which clusters have the greatest number of cards? This is a clue to which actions people sensed were most substantial.

Which clusters have the greatest mix of colors (actions were written on a different color of cards for each **Strategic Direction**)? This can reveal which actions are likely to have the widest impact.

Each cluster is then **named** by the group, beginning with the one with the most cards. The name describes the action called for by the cards in each cluster.

After a final reflection on the actions, noting which are most substantial, which are the most catalytic, which are necessary supporting actions, the group reviews the implications of these actions for the organization and the participants. Then a chart of the *Systematic Actions* is prepared, with the most catalytic action placed in the center.

Drawing Up an Implementation Timeline

Eighty-seven per cent [of the companies that participated in his survey] report feelings of disappointment and frustration with their systems [of strategic planning]. Fifty-nine percent [of these] attribute their discontent to difficulties encountered in the implementation of plans.

Daniel H. Gray

ToP Strategic Planning does not end with naming the **Systematic Actions** that are necessary to achieve the **Strategic Directions**. It goes on to clarify the who, how, what, why, where and when of each of those actions.

The first step is to determine the priority of the **Systematic Actions**. This is often done using a reflective conversation that refreshes the group's memory of the actions, especially if a night or more has passed since the last time they looked at the actions chart. Sometimes prioritizing is done in the reflection at the end of the **Systematic Actions Workshop**. In prioritizing the actions, the group determines which should be implemented in the first quarter of the year, which in the second, third and fourth quarters. The criteria for selection are:

Which are the most urgent actions?

Which are the easiest to accomplish and will therefore generate momentum?

Which actions will catalyze, or pave the way for several others?

Once the actions to be implemented in the first quarter are identified, they are divided up among teams. Team selection is important here. Depending on the organization, it's structure, the focus of the planning and the makeup of the group, the teams might consist of volunteers according to interest, they might be assigned by the superior present or be formed according to existing departmental responsibilities. The Texaco Story in Chapter 3 provides a good illustration of the values to be considered in constituting the teams at this point. The most critical value in team configuration is that the teams understand themselves to be responsible for implementing the action. They are not making decisions for someone else to carry out.

Each team will generally have one to three actions to work on. For each action, the team fills out an *implementation brief*. This form helps them to think through each step required to complete the action. Groups decide who will do each step and when, what resources will be required, and how the completion of the action will be measured. During this process, team members refer to their personal schedules, making appointments, scheduling meetings and phone calls, etc.

As teams work on the *implementation briefs*, the facilitator places a large timeline chart at the front of the wall, depicting the next three months, divided into weeks. The actions to be implemented in the coming quarter are listed down the left hand side of the chart. The teams are asked to write each of the implementing steps for each action on a card, including the names of those involved in the step. They also write a card describing the victory that will be achieved by the completion of that action. The victory cards are placed at the right hand side of the timeline, with each implementing step placed on the timeline in the week in which it will occur.

When all the teams have finished and placed their implementing steps on the timeline, the total group gathers to reflect. Each team reports on their implementation plans, and the group begins to see how they interface, complementing or contradicting each other. Adjustments are made, such as synchronizing or phasing related implementation steps so that they empower each other rather than conflict with each other. For example, if two teams scheduled major corporate events on the same day, they would decide which of the two should come first in terms of how they affect each other. They would then schedule these events so that they complement each other in relationship to the overall plan. This reflection and revision process helps cement the group as one big team, each playing their part in implementing the total plan, which they have created together, rather than a lot of small teams, each with their own agendas.

The *Implementation Timeline* is drawn up in a chart to be included in the final document. This will serve as the checkpoint for future review sessions.

The *ToP Strategic Planning Process* typically closes with a reflection upon the whole planning process that includes the process, the product and what has happened to the group during the process. It is in this reflection that the group members generally recognize that they have not only created a plan that they believe will win, but they also have become a team, committed and motivated to see the plan through together.

Summary

The *ToP Strategic Planning Process* has five steps:

1. Mapping Out the **Practical Vision**,
2. Analyzing the **Underlying Contradictions**,
3. Setting the **Strategic Directions**,
4. Designing the **Systematic Actions**, and
5. Drawing up the **Implementation Timeline**.

IMPLEMENTATION BRIEF

Date _____

_____
Accomplishment Title

90 DAY INTENT (What and Why)

IMPLEMENTATION STEPS (How)	WHO	WHEN

COORDINATOR:

TEAM MEMBERS:

Ordering the data in a Practical Vision Workshop.

Plenary Session of an Underlying Contradictions Workshop.

Naming the categories in a Strategic Directions Workshop.

Teams report their Action Steps in an Implementation Timeline Workshop.

Facilitator leads the evaluation of a *ToP Strategic Planning Workshop.*

Each of these five steps includes the three fundamental *ToP* methods:

1. the *ToP Focused Conversation Method*
2. the *ToP Workshop Method*
3. the *ToP Event Planning and Orchestration Techniques*

Each step, or session of the *ToP Strategic Planning Process* consists of a *ToP workshop* which elicits objective data and intuitive insights from the participants and weaves these together into a picture that is broader and deeper than any one person, or even a small group of top executives could have produced.

The use of *ToP focused conversations* at various points throughout the process allows the group to stand back and learn from what it has just accomplished. These points are usually at the beginning and end of each session, and also at transition points between teamwork and total group (plenary) sessions. This is immensely valuable in that the group discerns patterns and directions that cannot be seen from the perspective of one team or department. The whole picture comes into focus, giving each participant a more comprehensive understanding of the organization, the plan that is emerging and his or her role in it. This is a critical part in developing the sense of ownership, commitment and sense of total responsibility that is generated by *ToP* methods.

The *ToP event planning and orchestration techniques* are used to tailor each *ToP Strategic Planning Session* to the specific needs of the group, based upon variables such as:

- the structure and operating style of the organization,
- the size and composition of the group,

109

- the time frame of the session,
- the setting of the event, and
- the particular focus and intent of the planning.

The interaction of individuals, teams and the total group is choreographed to build in maximum participation and sense of ownership of the whole plan. There is no fixed pattern; each group requires customized attention. However, skilled use of these techniques is critical to the creation of the plan and the development of team spirit and commitment that will guarantee the successful implementation of the plan.

Our employees not only made contributions, they provided countless suggestions, tactics and proposals to improve our operations both short-term and long-term.

Robert C. McCrystal
President and CEO
American Cablevision Company

The sixty participants, representing federal, state, regional and local agencies, as well as the private sector, certainly departed the workshop with a spirit of cooperative effort to enhance the economic development viability of the State.

Richard D. Cole
Commissioner
Department of Local
Government
State of Kentucky

We spent less than a month creating plans that took several months with previous methods.

Dr. William T. Sackett
Vice President
Corporate Technology Center
Honeywell

These conferences over a period of time have resulted in a better understanding of customer needs. As a result, the marketing team has been able to achieve a 15% or more cumulative growth rate. The strength of the program came from building the format together with the [ToP facilitators] for the results we wanted and participating as co-facilitators in our own conference.

Marketing Manager
Indofil Chemicals Company
India

The next chapter will demonstrate the use of the *Technology of Participation* for leadership training and development.

CHAPTER 8

ToP Leadership Development

> *More and more companies are now saying that what they want is leadership. Not old-fashioned bureaucratic managers. . . . But leaders, real leaders.*
>
> Executive Searcher
Korn Ferry

> *Managers control. Leaders create commitment.*
>
> John H. Zenger
Management Consultant

As the manager's role has evolved from that of administration and control to facilitation and leadership, *ToP* methods have proven highly effective in meeting this need in two ways. 1) Training in the basic *ToP* methods provides facilitation skills to managers and supervisors at all levels within an organization. Furthermore, these skills tend to "rub off" onto those not trained in them, but who participate in participative problem-solving and planning sessions. 2) Secondly, *ToP* methods are highly effective as training tools to help participants understand and practically apply new concepts and skills for effective leadership.

ToP Methods as Leadership Skills

Many organizations that have used *ToP* methods for strategic planning or action planning have gone on to train their own staff in *ToP* methods, thereby incorporating the *ToP* into their ongoing operating patterns. Several examples are mentioned in this book, including Hughes Tool (Chapter 2), and Texaco (Chapter 3).

These organizations discover, as the *ToP* methods become part of the day-to-day planning and problem-solving process at every level of operations, that leadership skills begin to grow and individuals and teams become self-managing. By participating in frequent planning and problem-solving sessions, employees begin to pick up these skills and use them at their own work stations. Because they know their input is valued, they offer it freely, rather than expecting someone else to recognize and solve problems that arise.

Some of the most frequently mentioned leadership qualities sought by corporate executives today are:

- visionary thinking,
- excellent communication skills,
- ability to generate motivation and commitment,
- integrity,
- action oriented, and
- ability to manage change.

These are also among the benefits most often ascribed to *ToP* methods.

Like all *ToP* applications, training in *ToP* methods is custom designed for each client. However, the most common components of facilitator training include training in the methods described in Part II:

- the *ToP Focused Conversation Method*
- the *ToP Workshop Method*
- the *ToP Event Planning and Orchestration Techniques*.

Additional components frequently included are training in:

- the *ToP Strategic Planning Process*
- the *ToP Action Planning Process*
- the *ToP Seminar Method*
- the *ToP Presentation Preparation Technique*

The training process, as you might expect, is participative. A typical training module would follow these steps:

- a **demonstration** of the method to be learned;
- a **reflection** upon the methods that were used, the results achieved and the effect they had on the group;
- a **presentation** on the procedures used in applying the method;
- individual or team **preparation** of an application of the method;
- **practice** in applying the method; and
- **evaluation** and reflection on the practice.

To illustrate, imagine a training module on the *ToP Workshop Method*. The module begins with a **demonstration** workshop. The topic or focus is one that is relevant to the participants, but not emotionally charged or an issue of great urgency. They need to remain detached enough from the content to be able to observe the process. Topics like team building, planning a departmental celebration or designing the ideal work environment serve as good demonstration topics. The trainer plays the role of facilitator and the trainees participate in creating the product.

Following the demonstration, a *focused conversation* allows the group to rehearse the demonstration workshop, evaluate its effectiveness and **reflect** upon how the methods used brought about the results. They also note the effect of the method upon the group and upon themselves as individuals.

A **presentation** lays out the step-by-step procedures of facilitating a *ToP workshop*. The demonstration workshop serves as a reference point for illustrating various procedures and "tricks of the trade." Worksheets to assist in preparation of a workshop are distributed and a question and answer period allows participants to fine-tune their understanding.

Individually or in teams, the participants are given time to **prepare** to lead a workshop. In most cases, the topic is predetermined or arrived at by a consensus of the group. Occasionally, it is left up to the individual or team to decide.

The **practice** workshop can be conducted in several ways:

- One person (volunteer or assigned) can lead the entire workshop.
- The workshop can be broken into five parts (context, brainstorm, order, name and reflect) and different participants can lead each part.
- Several practice workshops can be conducted simultaneously in teams.

The size of the group, the number of trainers and the time frame of the training session all determine how the practice workshops will be conducted. However, those participating as well as those practicing facilitating gain much practical experience of the tricks to have up one's sleeve and the pitfalls to avoid in facilitation.

The **evaluation,** usually done in the form of a *focused conversation,* reinforces and enhances the learnings from the practice workshop. As those who practiced facilitating and those who participated share their observations, experiences and learnings with each other the entire group's understanding of the method is broadened and deepened.

Like any skill, facilitating *ToP* methods is best learned through practice. Having participated in a training session gives a person the theoretical and practical understanding of the method and how it works. The next step is to put it to work. When managers or supervisors from the same organization are trained together, they often choose to work together to prepare workshops or other *ToP* methods applications until each feels confident enough on their own. The more the methods are used, the easier they become and the more the facilitator will discover their adaptability to many situations.

Top Methods as Training Tools

Training people to facilitate with *ToP* methods provides valuable leadership skills that can be disseminated throughout the organization at all levels. However, *ToP* methods can also be used as valuable learning tools to help people master leadership concepts and techniques from other sources. Several examples will be given later in this chapter.

Why are *ToP* methods so useful for training? Studies show that any material is best mastered when the learner talks about what he or she has learned. The *ToP Focused Conversation Method* enables a group of people to talk about what they have read, observed or experienced, thus objectifying the information. They then evaluate its impact upon themselves and make a decision about their relationship to the information (whether or not it is true, the best use for it, etc.).

The *ToP Seminar Method* is an excellent tool for group study. It involves making a chart, which is a visual image of a book or article, then engaging in an extended *focused conversation* on the chart as a way to understand the author's message and its implications for the group.

"Tell me, I forget. Show me, I remember. Involve me, I understand." This Chinese proverb explains why the *ToP Workshop Method* is an effective training tool. When new data is presented, the best way to understand how and why it works is to try it in a practical situation. In *ToP* leadership training programs, a seminar on a book, such as *Creating Excellence* or a practicum on a new technique is often followed by a workshop in which the participants corporately build a plan for putting the new concepts into practice in their work place. Thus, the training moves from theory to practice to effective application, rather than just being filed away in the back of participants' minds as an interesting idea that might find a use someday.

The *Top Leadership Development Lab*

Many leadership development programs have been designed using the *ToP* methods to train managers in a wide variety of leadership skills and concepts. One of the best examples is provided by the Taj Group of Hotels, part of the Tata Group of Companies, one of the largest and most respected industrial houses in India. Under the leadership of Managing Director Ajit Kerkar, the Taj Group of Hotels has expanded forty-fold in just fifteen years.

The group has a tradition of developing leaders from the ranks, with many senior executives having risen from entry level positions. Because rapid expansion required that the Taj Group of Hotels accelerate the development of talented middle managers, V.S. Mahesh, Vice President of Human Resources Development, called upon the ICA: India to design a program to train young "fast track" managers considered by their superiors to have executive potential. Mahesh is described as a visionary "agent of change," who sees a participative environment as the management style of the future. He found in the *Technology of Participation* the skills needed to make that future happen.

Mahesh explained that the program was intended "to accelerate the process of development of our young people. Some of our older managers had come up through a trial and error process. At that time there were no business schools and you had people who were hired for technical excellence and had to move up into management positions," he observed. "We wanted to know what we could do with young people who seem to exhibit that potential now, so that from the organization's side we could meet them half way and make them consciously realize that they need to develop their leadership skills and hone their leadership styles."

The program was designed to support Mahesh's philosophy that management must enable all employees to achieve their highest potential. "If I can get the entire management at all levels to accept that their success, their department's success, and the organization's success is critically dependent on how they help people working with them to develop as fast as possible and to reach their full potential, then I would be happy," Mahesh explained. "And if this comes genuinely from a leader and he does everything right to help his people reach peak performance and operate at that level, then I think that nothing can stop this organization."

The *Leadership Development Lab* that ICA: India designed for the Taj Group of Hotels consisted of three one-week modules, with four to eight weeks between each session so that participants could put their newly acquired skills to the test in the workplace. About 30 "fast track" general manager candidates attended the sessions. A similar 2-day program was held to acquaint department heads and senior managers with the training program in which their staff were participating.

Module I of the *Leadership Development Lab* covered Individual Development Skills, Module II addressed Team Building Skills, and Module III focused on Culture Building Skills. The format included demonstrations and practice of all of the **ToP** methods as well as a wide variety of other resources. Because the lab was developed in cooperation with Mahesh, several sessions were devoted to specific issues and concerns of the Taj Group's staff, such as time management and culture analysis. Each module ended with a written and oral evaluation and assignments for skill practice during the interim period.

Module I: Individual Development—The Leader as Innovator

The focus of Module I was on individual development, or the leader as innovator. The five days included:

- several study sessions on the leadership skills called for by Hickman and Silva in the book *Creating Excellence,*
- study and application of the Myers-Briggs personality types,
- excercises from *A Whack on the Side of the Head* and *The Possible Human* which demonstrated to participants their own creative and intuitive capacities,

```
┌─────────────────────────────────────────────────────────┐
│              Leadership Development Lab                  │
└─────────────────────────────────────────────────────────┘
```

MODULE 1	MODULE 2	MODULE 3
INDIVIDUAL SKILLS	*TEAM SKILLS*	*CULTURE SKILLS*
Personality Profile	Workshop Practice	Culture Analysis
Charting Method	Listening Skills	Situational Leadership
Creativity Skills	Discussion Method	Mind Mapping
Individual Problem Solving	Space Design	Presentation Skills
Basic Workshop	Facilitation Skills	Maslow Application
Supervision Skills	Effective Meetings	Strategy Design
Time Management	Seminar Leading	MBO/KRA Targets
	Team Evaluation	

- portions of the videos, *In Search of Excellence* and *Everything You Ever Wanted to Know About Supervision* provided images of innovative leadership styles,
- two sessions focusing on time management, based upon the work of Peter Drucker and
- Training in the **ToP Seminar Method, Workshop Method, Action Planning Method** and the **Strategic Planning Process** was provided and used in several of the sessions. For example, the **ToP Seminar Method** was used to study *Creating Excellence* and the **ToP Strategic Planning Process** was used to develop plans for creating excellence in several aspects of the Taj Group's operations.

Module I ended with a reflection and evaluation. Participants returned to their jobs for three weeks to practice their new skills and to implement the plans they had created.

Module II: Team Development—The Leader as Facilitator

The focus of Module II was on team development, and the leadership style of the facilitator. Following is a summary of the components of this module.

- A review of the participants' experience in applying the learnings of Module I on the job was conducted.

- Practice workshops and seminars were led by participants. These were evaluated and critiqued by their colleagues.
- The management skills of sensitivity, versatility and patience described in *Creating Excellence* were studied.
- Exercises based on Abraham Maslow's hierarchy of needs, Frederick Herzberg's motivational theory and John Kenneth Galbraith's work on power helped ground these concepts for the participants.
- Further segments of the video *In Search of Excellence* provided helpful images of these leadership skills in action.
- The *ToP Focused Conversation Method* was taught in this module, and subsequent conversations for the whole group were led by participants. The *ToP Event Planning and Orchestration Techniques* (particularly the *STEPS* for *ToP* events, described in Chapter 6) were emphasized. Workshops were conducted on designing the team space, planning an eventful team outing and designing a meeting. A presentation on the role and style of the facilitator was followed by a workshop on how to develop versatility in the staff.
- *The ToP Strategic Planning Process* was used to develop different plans for team development within the Taj Group of Hotels.

Once again, following reflection and evaluation, the participants returned to their jobs for three weeks to put their skills and plans to work.

Module III: Developing Organizational Culture—The Leader as Motivator
Module III stressed the development of organizational culture and the role of leader as motivator, recognizing that the culture of a company is reshaped by each new generation of leaders. Included were:

- An analysis of the Taj Group's culture which revealed the essential role that management plays in transmitting values throughout the organization.
- Study and practice of various leadership styles and techniques including the book, *Leadership and the One Minute Manager,* Roger Harrison's *Strategies for a New Age,* Management By Objectives techniques of personal and departmental target setting and further work with Maslow's hierarchy of needs and Galbraith's work on power.
- Exercises included mind mapping and creative thinking.
- Training in the *ToP Presentation Preparation method.*
- Three videos served as topics for *Focused Conversations:* a segment from *In Search of Excellence* seeded the session on culture analysis, *Twelve O'Clock High* provided images for the session on leadership styles and *The Global Brain* launched a closing personal growth retreat.

V. S. Mahesh worked closely with the ICA in designing this program. His efforts ensured that the lab would address some specific concerns of the Taj Group of Hotels. His primary interest was that participants identify management's task as that of moving employees toward self-actualization, toward greater self-initiation and innovation.

The participants' comments about the lab reflected their enthusiasm.

> *These three weeks have been a great learning experience. They have given me a lot of self-confidence, a sense of perfection, and taught me to be results-oriented.*

> *The three weeks have shown me that nothing is impossible if I want to do it, that I have potential, and that a manager and a leader are two different things.*

> *The course has provided me with many leadership skills, the art of facilitating a workshop, the strength that lies in team building, and the importance of strategic planning.*

Perhaps the greatest enthusiasm was expressed by Vice President Mahesh, who commented that "most programs do not lead to the same kind of togetherness, commitment, and a kind of synergistic force that gets produced when people of good quality are engaged in good quality interaction, and the context or the environment is also attended to properly. The young people got highly motivated, they got a direction toward what they need to do for self-development. And I think the unique feature was that at the end of each week's program they came up with a very specific action plan, irrespective of what the rest of the world would do for them. More often than not people attend programs and come back and say 'My boss didn't help me' and 'So-and-so didn't give me support.' But by our very definition a leader has to be pro-active, and pro-active people don't give reactive excuses. So at the end of the week they went ahead like pro-active people and planned what they were going to do. This happened for each program and it improved both the skills they picked up and the confidence they had in transferring that into working conditions."

As a result of the *Leadership Development Lab*, Mahesh commissioned the ICA: India to set up workshops for the Taj Group's department chiefs and senior managers. "As a trainer I would be very reluctant to claim that there is a causal relationship between the training and its impact," Mahesh explained. "I do believe that this has had a tremendous impact as a catalyst to generate a significant number of things." Mahesh went on to say that all indications to date are that the vast majority of the participants have been recognized by both superiors and subordinates as having demonstrated the quality that in the Taj Group's culture is most highly prized, a people-oriented style.

Developing leaders at all levels, with far-sighted management at the helm, is enabling the Taj Group of Hotels to keep up in an era of fast-paced change and expansion.

The three-week *Leadership Development Lab* is one of the most intensive and extensive programs using *ToP* methods for training within an organization. There are many shorter versions, using many of the same resources. The three week program was used to illustrate the scope and depth, as well as versatility of *ToP* methods for leadership development.

CHAPTER 9

ToP Mission and Philosophy Retreat

Mission supplies the form to which strategy can give substance.
David K. Hurst
Executive Vice President
Russelsteel, Inc.

Our endeavor is to forge a shared view of reality that will serve the organization members as a base for day-to-day decision making.
Roger Harrison
Strategies for a New Age

For several reasons organizations are funneling increasing time and energy into developing corporate missions and philosophies. Emphasis over recent years on corporate culture and the role it plays in creating excellence within organizations is one reason. Mission and philosophy are key elements of corporate culture.

A second reason is that enlightened leadership recognizes that employees' understanding of the organization's mission generally connects that mission to their own personal sense of purpose. That connection yields enhanced motivation, commitment and fulfillment.

But perhaps the biggest reason is change. The rapidity and radicality of change in the environment, the marketplace, the workforce combine to force organizations to rehearse, re-examine and sometimes recreate their mission and philosophy.

Amid so much change there has also been much discussion about the relationship between mission and strategy. One critic of "strategic management" charges that this approach is too short-ranged and ignores the concept of mission. Roger Harrison regards strategic thinking as "a search for meaning." The emerging consensus is that sound strategy is not enough. Strategy must be founded upon a clearly stated mission that is understood by all members of an organization.

ToP methods have pioneered in this concept and have evolved in response to this new consensus. In the *ToP Strategic Planning Process,* the **Practical Vision** session is a way of rehearsing the corporate mission and then stating its practical manifestation over the next five years. The result of this session is an alignment of members around that vision setting the stage for the construction of a concerted strategic plan. In many *ToP Strategic Planning* events, a **Song/Story/Symbol Workshop** is conducted to focus the group's understanding of the corporate mission and philosophy.

Increasingly, however, organizations find that simple rehearsal of an existing corporate mission statement is impossible during the **Practical Vision** session. Rather, they have to create or recreate it. Some organizations never even had a written mission statement, but operated on assumptions. They are now discovering the importance of a commonly understood mission statement. Organizations that do have such statements often find that due to changes in their environment, product line or organizational structure, their statements are no longer meaningful.

In response to these needs, *ToP* methods have assisted organizations in developing or re-empowering their corporate mission and philosophy. Again, several designs have been developed, tailored to the specific needs of clients. In this chapter we will describe a typi-

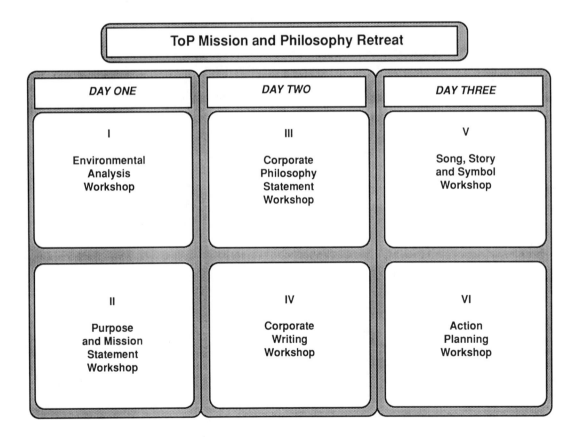

ToP Mission and Philosophy Retreat

DAY ONE	DAY TWO	DAY THREE
I Environmental Analysis Workshop	III Corporate Philosophy Statement Workshop	V Song, Story and Symbol Workshop
II Purpose and Mission Statement Workshop	IV Corporate Writing Workshop	VI Action Planning Workshop

cal *ToP Mission and Philosophy Retreat* consisting of some of the most commonly used components.

The *ToP Mission and Philosophy Retreat* has six sessions that are usually spread over three days. Since the process involves creating distance from the day-to-day operations and stepping back to look at the organization from a larger perspective, it is helpful to hold the retreat away from the company facility. A hotel, country club or retreat center are common choices. Whenever possible, it is best to provide outdoor space for walking and talking or walking and reflecting. Space in a natural setting adds a dimension to the retreat that enhances the tone of the dialogue and therefore, the product. In the same way, a somewhat relaxed schedule with breaks long enough to take advantage of the space puts people in a frame of mind that helps in this particular task.

Session I: Environmental Analysis

. . . Organization purpose is not simply decided by it members, but is in large part "given" by its membership in the larger system. The process of discovery is partly internal to the organization, involving an inner search for values and meaning. It also has an external aspect, that of discovering meaning through the transactions of the organization with its environment. Viewed in this way, a primary task of the leadership is the discovery of the organization's place and purpose in the world. And every event in its history can be viewed as part of a lesson.

Roger Harrison
Strategies for a New Age

Like Janus, the Roman god of the threshold, the organization looks forward to the future and back to the past. Mission prospects while strategy retrospects. The two meet in the present. Thus the organization grows (learns) by expanding its perceived environment—by recognizing and processing opportunities.

David K. Hurst
Why Strategic Management is Bankrupt

Context

Following an opening context, usually given by the C.E.O. or senior executive responsible for the retreat, the first session begins with an **Environmental Analysis Workshop**. Sometimes known as **Trends Analysis** or a **Wall of Wonder**, this workshop is very effective at providing the group with an enlarged perspective from which to examine its current situation.

This workshop, therefore, serves as a contextual session for the entire retreat.

ENVIRONMENTAL ANALYSIS				
EVENTS	Beginning of Organization	Present	Future	TRENDS
WORLD				
INDUSTRY				
ORGANIZATION				

A large wall chart holds a timeline that begins the year the organization began. The present is at the center of the timeline and the future is projected as many years forward as there are in the history of the organization.

Down the left hand side of the chart are three categories:

- WORLD,
- INDUSTRY, and
- ORGANIZATION.

At the right of the chart is a column entitled "Trends."

Brainstorm

Participants are asked to write down one event that impacted the WORLD for each year on the timeline. If the organization is very old, the years are grouped into five or ten year blocks and events are written for each time block. If the timeline predates the memory of some members of the group, they can write things they know from history and skip periods about which they have no information. For the future years, the group is encouraged to use its imagination and write predictions, visions, guesses, hopes and dreams.

After events are listed, participants are asked to mark the three most earth-shaking events on their list and write them on cards. If the group is large, small teams of two or three can be formed. In this case, each team reviews each member's key events and selects three events from among them. The year the event took place is marked on the back of the card and the cards are passed forward to the facilitator.

Order

The facilitator reads out the event on each card and places it on the wall under the year in which it occurred. When all the cards are on the wall chart, the facilitator asks two or three reflective questions, such as:

- What strikes you as you look at this chart?
- Are there any events you had completely forgotten about?
- What surprises you about the events in the future?

The same process is repeated for the next category, INDUSTRY. This category refers to the industry that the organization is part of, such as the housing industry or the aerospace industry. A school, for example, might analyze the education industry or profession. A government agency might analyze state government. The facilitator decides the appropriate name for this category in consultation with the personnel responsible for the retreat.

These events are written on cards of a different color than those on which WORLD events were written. After placing these cards on the wall chart and asking a few more questions, the process is repeated for the organization itself.

The facilitator then guides a *ToP Focused Conversation* on the chart that the group has just created. The questions might be:

- Looking over the whole chart, where do you see great clusters of events when a lot seemed to be going on all at once?
- Where are there gaps, or slow periods?
- What relationships do you see between what goes on in the world and the industry we are in? Between the world and our company? Between our company and the industry of which we are a part? How do we respond?
- Where do you see major shifts or turning points? (The facilitator marks these on the wall chart)
- What would you say this was a shift **from** and what was it a shift **to**?

Name

The naming step of this workshop happens as the conversation reaches the decisional level.

- As you look at the time periods delineated by the shifts we just identified, what names would you give to each period? Finish the phrase, "This was a time of. . . ." The facilitator writes these names on the chart above each time period.
- Now look at the board from left to right. What trends do you see emerging in the WORLD? In our INDUSTRY? In our ORGANIZATION? These are listed on the chart in the TRENDS column.
- What are the implications of these trends for our organization?
- We have used our memories, imagination and creativity to create quite an art form here. What name would you give to this work of art?

Evaluation

- Take a mental step back now. Instead of sitting in your chair looking at this work of art, imagine that you are outside this room looking in at the group sitting here. Describe what you have seen going on. What did we do this morning?
- What surprised you?
- What happened to us as a group as we did this?
- If you have lunch today with someone who wasn't here this morning and they ask you what you did here, what will you tell them?

The **Environmental Analysis Workshop** sets the stage for the **Mission and Philosophy Workshops** that follow.

Session II: The Purpose and Mission Statement Workshop

Context

The **purpose** of an organization is a statement of it's reason for being. It answers the question of "WHY are we in existence?"

The **mission** of an organization defines its role or task. It answers the question of "WHAT do we do to fulfill our purpose?"

The **philosophy** of an organization is a statement of the values it holds in carrying out its mission and fulfilling its purpose. It answers the question of "HOW do we do things here?"

To further understand these concepts, the group studies Roger Harrison's *Strategies for a New Age,* focusing on the concepts of alignment and attunement.

This session identifies the key elements of the organization's purpose and mission. The philosophy will be articulated in the next session. Each of these statements will be written up in the corporate writing session.

Brainstorm

The facilitator reads a series of questions and asks the participants to write down their answers to them as they are read.

- An extra-terrestrial comes to Earth. It points to everything it sees (like a bus station, an electric power plant, a school, a park, your factory) and asks, ''What's that for?'' What will you tell it?
- Your son or daughter ask you why you work for your company rather than another. What is your answer?
- 1000 years from now a history book of the 21st Century is uncovered. It has a section on your company's contribution to society. What does it say?
- If you were going to spend the rest of your life working with your company, and the only thing you would be remembered for is what you do there, what would you want your company to be known for?
- What would the world lose if your company quit operating tomorrow?

In teams of two or three, participants share their answers with each other. They list the words, images or concepts that came up more than once. Each team selects the three that were mentioned most often or which seem most critical. These are written on cards.

Order

The cards are passed forward and clustered according to similar *content*.

Name

Each cluster is named by completing the sentence, ''The purpose of this organization is. . . .''

Evaluate

A short *focused conversation* is led to evaluate the data.

- Which cluster has the most cards? The least?
- Did you hear anything that surprised you?
- Which cluster would you throw away?
- Which one would you defend with your life?

This data provides grist for the team writing the purpose statement in Session IV. Next is the **Mission Statement Workshop**.

Brainstorm

Participants are asked to list all of the stakeholders in their organization. They are prompted by questions like :

- To what people, organizations or institutions is this organization related?
- Who has a stake in this organization?
- Who is the organization dependent upon?
- Who is dependent upon the organization?
- Who would miss the organization if it ceased to exist?
- Who would be pleased to see it succeed?

In order to quickly determine the stakeholders, the facilitator asks, "What is the biggest category of stakeholders on your list? As answers are given, the facilitator asks each respondent to write their answer on a card and send it forward. Only one card is written for each category of stakeholders. These are placed in columns on the wall.

After several major stakeholders are identified, the facilitator asks, "Who has a stakeholder on their list that they think no one else has thought of?" These answers are shared, then written on cards and added to the list on the wall.

Order

When the group is satisfied that all the stakeholders have been named, the categories are reviewed to eliminate redundancy. For example, several types of customers might be grouped into one category called "customers."

Brainstorm

The group is divided into three or four teams of 5–8 members each. Each individual lists responsibilities the organization has toward each stakeholder. They select the one or two most critical responsibilities for each stakeholder.

The team shares its selected items and selects two or three for each stakeholder. These are written on cards for the plenary, marking the stakeholder category on the back of each card.

Order

The cards are placed on the wall under the name of the stakeholder category indicated on the back of each card.

126

Name

The facilitator reads through the responsibilities under each stakeholder category and asks for questions of clarity from the group. Then the facilitator asks which words or phrases from the cards most aptly describe the organization's responsibility to that stakeholder. These are underlined for use by the team writing the mission statement.

Evaluate

A scribe is asked to take notes on the evaluation conversation, so that insights gained can be added to the data for the writing team.

- Which are the most critical relationships for our future?
- Which have the most to say about our deep purpose?
- What of all this should definitely not be left out of our Purpose and Mission statement?
- Who are the most important stakeholders for our future?

All the data from this workshop, including notes on the evaluation conversation are carefully collected and saved for the corporate writing workshop.

Session III: The Corporate Philosophy Statement Workshop

> *Every excellent company we studied is clear on what it stands for, and takes the process of value shaping seriously. In fact, we wonder whether it is possible to be an excellent company without clarity on values and without having the right sorts of values.*
>
> Peters and Waterman
> *In Search of Excellence*

Context

The context for the **Corporate Philosophy Statement Workshop** is set by the Disneyland segment of the videotape, *In Search of Excellence*. This fifteen minute segment illustrates a company that goes to extremes to ensure that all of its employees understand and act out the values and philosophy of the company in everything they do. A focused conversation follows the video, enabling the group to reflect upon what they have learned and the implications for their own organization.

The *Corporate Culture Triangle* may be introduced as an additional tool that helps the group interpret the Disney video and analyze their own strengths and weaknesses.

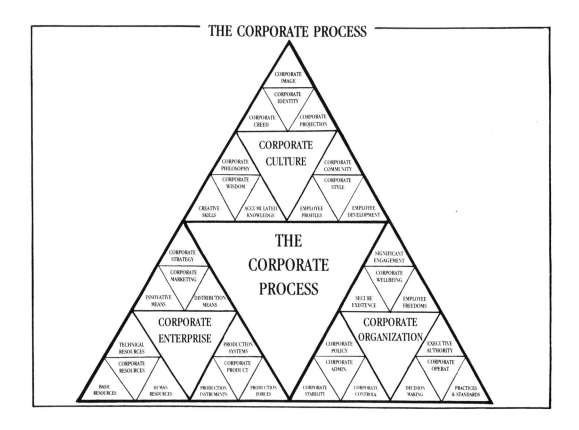

The corporate philosophy is a set of values that defines how things are done within an organization. This includes:

how the organization relates to its customers,

how it relates to its product or service,

how members of the organization relate to each other,

what is valued (this may include attitudes, behavior, style of dress, etc.), and

what is discouraged.

The more clearly the corporate philosophy is articulated and communicated, the better all employees are able to understand and act appropriately in accordance with it.

Brainstorm

Participants now list the values they believe the organization holds in the following arenas:

Leadership,

Teamwork,

Communication,

Recognition,

Accountability,

Planning,

Problem solving,

Coordination,

Innovation,

Corporate image,

Things we always do,

Things we never do,

Things we look for in recruits,

Things we show to visitors,

One thing you would change,

The last thing we should ever give up, and

Our story about why people come to our organization and why they leave it.

Order

Individuals mark the five values from their entire list that they believe to be most critical for the organization to honor in the future.

In teams, individuals share their marked values and each team selects ten to twelve to share with the entire group. These are written on cards.

The whole group regathers and the facilitator asks each team to select what they believe are the three most critical values from among their cards and to number those three. Each team then sends forward the card that represents the most important value for the organization to guard in the future.

The facilitator then asks the teams to send forward any remaining important values if they are not already represented by other cards on the board. As the cards are put up, they are grouped into columns by similar *values*. The facilitator asks if there are still any cards out of the three most important that do not fit into any of the columns. If there are, these are sent forward and put on the board.

Each column is then given a holding title describing the value named in the column. The teams are asked to mark their remaining cards with the symbol of the column into which they fit.

Name

When all the cards are passed forward and placed in their appropriate columns, the facilitator reads all the cards in each column and the group reaches a consensus on the final name for the value described by the cards in each column.

Evaluate

A brief focused conversation is held to evaluate the work, reflecting upon the values that have been articulated and what they say about the organization now and in the future.

The data is collected and saved for the corporate writing workshop.

Session IV: The Corporate Writing Workshop

1. Everyone operates out of images of themselves and the world.
2. Peoples' images determine their behavior.
3. Images can be changed by new messages.
4. When images are changed, behavior changes.

ICA
Imaginal Education Curriculum

Context

A brief presentation is made on the power of images in learning and communicating. This presentation elaborates on the four points above, derived from Kenneth Boulding's *The Image.*

A *focused conversation* helps the group ground these four points. The group is then divided into two teams. One team writes the purpose and mission statements. These are best written by one team because they often tend to overlap if written separately. The second team writes the corporate philosophy statement. The facilitator may give instructions to both teams before dispersing them or a facilitator may work with each team. A few guidelines are provided about writing concise statements with power and precision. Then the teams go to work.

Brainstorm

In teams, the group reviews all data provided on the **Purpose and Mission Statement** charts or the values chart from the **Philosophy Statement Workshop.** Each participant writes a statement that they believe holds together the consensus of the group. Generally, the purpose statement is one sentence, the mission statement is a paragraph or a series of statements of what the organization does and the philosophy statement is a list of values the organizations stands behind.

Order

When each individual has written a statement, these are shared and the team reflects upon what they heard. Usually, words, phrases or sentences from several people's writings are found to capture different aspects of the whole statement particularly well.

Name

These well articulated pieces are then woven together into one statement that expresses the consensus of the whole group.

The two teams come together to "check signals", sharing their statements with each other. This is a way of providing objectivity, which often gets lost when a small group focuses intensely on one thing. For example, when those who have worked on the values statement hear the work of the purpose and mission statement team, they often notice things that have been left out, underemphasized or overemphasized.

Each team makes comments and suggestions regarding the other team's work. Then the two teams regroup and refine their statements, taking into consideration the suggestions of the larger group.

Evaluate

At the final plenary, both statements are shared, condensed upon and celebrated. A *focused conversation* occasions reflection on the statements of the corporate purpose, mission and philosophy that the group has created. This tends to be a powerful moment. The group has, in effect, rededicated itself. Profound levels of excitement, commitment and energy are released as participants articulate their common mission and philosophy.

The conversation also enables reflection on the group's experience as they worked. Typically, this is a highly unifying experience. A new sense of team spirit and cohesive power is discovered. It is a fine time for a celebration.

Many *ToP Mission and Philosophy Retreats* end at this point, having created and celebrated the corporate Purpose, Mission and Philosophy Statements. However, one construct has two additional sessions that are worth describing, because each have many applications. These are the **Song, Story and Symbol Workshop** and the *Action Planning Workshop.*

Session V: Song, Story and Symbol Workshop

The **Song, Story and Symbol Workshop** has many applications and can be used in many *ToP* programs besides the *Mission and Philosophy Retreat.* It is frequently included in *ToP Strategic Planning Process* as a sixth session. It is included in this *Mission and Philosophy Retreat* as a prelude to the **Action Planning Workshop,** in which a plan will be built to communicate the purpose, mission and philosophy statements to all members of the organization.

Context

The task of this workshop is to create a song, a story and a symbol that communicate the self-understanding (mission and philosophy) of the organization to its members and to the world. This is done in three teams. At this point, a review of the presentation on images and behavior (given at the beginning of the **Corporate Writing Workshop**) is appropriate, since music, art and story-telling are especially effective media for freighting images.

Brainstorm

In this retreat, the brainstorm has already been done to a large extent. The data from the preceding workshops provides the data and the images needed to create the song, story and symbol. A *focused conversation* on the data from previous sessions might refresh the group's memory of some of the pieces that made up the whole event to date. The conversation might include some questions like:

- As you listened to the mission and value statements being read, what kind of music came to your mind? Or if you were going to read them with music in the background, what tunes or type of music would seem appropriate?
- Did any myths or historical epics, movements or figures come to your mind as you listened to the statements or as you worked in your teams?
- Did you see any graphic images as you worked on developing those statements, like geometric designs, patterns, or images of animals or nature? What were some of those images?

Order

The teams working on each product (song story and symbol) are designated before this conversation and one person from each team takes notes on the conversation. The teams then gather and review input that seems most appropriate for their particular task.

The **Song** team will consider the types of music that people suggested as appropriate background music to the reading of the mission and philosophy statements. Sometimes, song titles or phrases have come up in the process of writing the statements and these can also be considered as possible tunes. The team will also consider the content and style of the song lyrics. They may choose to simply express the corporate mission and/or philosophy, or they may choose to tell something of the history of the company in something like a ballad, describing how they arrived at this point and where they are going. By considering the tune and the lyrics together, they usually arrive at a consensus that seems to do justice to both. Then they write the song, much like they wrote the mission or philosophy statements.

The **Story** team takes into consideration any previous comments about mythological or historical events or figures. These can provide images, themes or frameworks around which to write the corporate story. They also may review in some detail the *Environmental Analysis* chart from Session I of the retreat, to collect vignettes from the organization's history. They decide upon the style of their story (eg. legend, science fiction documentary, etc.) and the central theme and characters. Then they set to writing.

The **Symbol** team reviews comments about graphic or visual images reported during the conversation, or any from teams in earlier working sessions. They may choose to do a visualization exercise as one member reads the mission and philosophy statements. It is perfectly legitimate to send ''spies'' to the song and story groups to find out if any of their ideas suggest images that might become part of the symbol. Once several images have been suggested, the team begins to get an intuitive sense of which ones seem to have the most power. Individuals begin to sketch their ideas and share them. Several images may be incorporated into one symbol, or they might merge together to form a new image altogether.

Name

The consensus process here is highly intuitive. Each team is engaging in corporate art. The teams may be formed voluntarily or by assignment. In either case, the individuals discover new talents in themselves and in their colleagues. The teams have fun, create meaning and further enhance their team spirit.

Evaluate

When each team has finished, the total group regathers and each team presents its art form. The song team sings the song and invites the rest of the group to join in. The story team reads the story and may even act it out, if appropriate. The symbol team presents the symbol with as much artistic flair as they can muster and explains it, if necessary. A *focused conversation* enables the group to process the art forms, so that each member identifies with each one, not just the one they helped to create. There is typically much enthusiasm and high spirit in this plenary. Because these art forms are built from the group's experience in the past few days, participants are excited to see their expenditure captured in these creative expressions.

At the same time, the question begins to emerge, ''How do we communicate our work to all the members of the organization so that they, too, can share in the ownership of this corporate mission and philosophy?'' In many cases the song, story and symbol become a part of that communication. In some cases they don't. However, answering that question is the intent of the last session in this retreat, the **Action Planning Workshop**.

Session VI: The Action Planning Workshop

The **Action Planning Workshop** is another *ToP* method that has a wide variety of applications. It is useful for planning short term projects or campaigns and for prioritizing the week's activities for a team or department. In the *ToP Mission and Philosophy Retreat* it is used to develop a plan for communicating the mission and philosophy statements to the membership of the organization who were not present at the retreat.

There are three basic phases of the **Action Planning Workshop.** They are:

1. Name the Victory,
2. Determine the Key Actions, and
3. Create the Calendar and Assignments.

These phases are carried out through the *ToP Workshop Method.*

Context

The context for the workshop is created participatively as the group names the victory they want to achieve. In this case, it is communicating the corporate mission and philosophy to the total membership. The group is asked to describe what that victory would look like, sound like, feel like, taste like. A visualization exercise can be used here. The object is to get as many specific images as possible of the desired objective. These images are put on the board, but not ordered.

The group then analyzes the current reality by listing internal strengths and weaknesses and external opportunities and threats involved in pursuing this victory. Notes on potential benefits and dangers are recorded on the board.

In response to the question, "What does the current reality reveal about the victory?" the group writes a statement articulating its commitment to the victory.

Brainstorm

Each individual brainstorms a list of actions to help accomplish the victory. They each select their best one, write it on a card and send it forward (this can be done by teams if the group is large).

Order

The cards are clustered according to similar *actions.* Individuals then mark the rest of their cards according to the cluster into which they fit and send them forward.

Name

Each cluster of actions is named. From these key action names, an overall name, slogan or visual image is discerned that describes the campaign that will accomplish the victory.

The next phase of the workshop is to create a calendar of scheduled actions and assignments. A wall-sized timeline is put up. The victory date is at the right end of the timeline. The key actions are listed down the left hand side of the chart. The timeline is divided into three sections: launch activity, ongoing activities and victory complete.

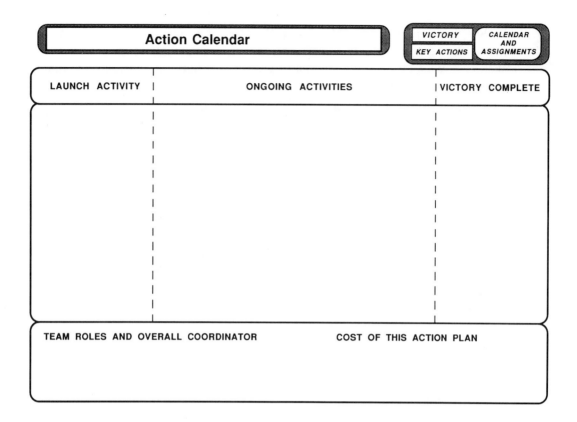

| LAUNCH ACTIVITY | ONGOING ACTIVITIES | VICTORY COMPLETE |

TEAM ROLES AND OVERALL COORDINATOR   **COST OF THIS ACTION PLAN**

The group is divided into teams, each taking one or two key actions. Using the cards in the key action cluster, they determine the steps to implementing the key action. They may use the cards as they are, discard some, combine some and make new ones as needed to ensure completion of the key action. The cards are placed along the timeline in the appropriate section (launch activity, ongoing activity or victory complete). For example, if one key action was to adopt the symbol created in the **Song, Story Symbol Workshop** as the official corporate logo, a launch activity might be an unveiling ceremony at which the new symbol would be introduced to appropriate audiences (eg. board of directors, shareholders, employees, etc.). Ongoing activities might include having the artwork commissioned to make the logo available for different uses (such as signs, stationery, calling cards, vehicle emblems, etc.). The completed victory might be the mounting of the new corporate logo at the entrance of the head office and issuing new stationery and calling cards bearing the logo all on one day.

Evaluate

When each team's actions are on the calendar, each team reports to the whole group on its actions. The group reviews the whole calendar, looking for points of conflict or convergence involving time or personnel. An overall coordinator is chosen. Leaders are also selected for each of the key actions. Finally, the cost of the action plan is estimated.

Some key actions that might come out of an **Action Planning Workshop** at the end of a *Mission and Philosophy Retreat* could include:

Debriefing events for each team or department. These might include sharing the results of the retreat as well as involving employees in some aspect of the retreat such as learning the new song or designing a variation of the symbol that is unique to their department;

Adopting the symbol as the new corporate logo;

Printing the corporate mission and philosophy statements in the employee handbook;

Designing a module for inclusion in new employee orientation sessions to help new employees understand the corporate mission and philosophy and know what it means to operate out of that understanding.

A brief *focused conversation* on the workshop itself allows the group to step back from the timeline and reflect upon their activity as a group and the implications the victory will have for their organization. This again broadens the group's perspective, reminding them that there are several key actions to accomplishing the victory. It takes them back to where they were when they began the workshop, reminding them of why they decided it necessary to communicate the corporate mission and philosophy to their membership to begin with. This kind of reflection after every stage of a workshop is extremely important, because in the midst of the workshop, people tend to get engrossed in the details of one particular part of the plan. The reflection brings them back to the big picture and enables them to restate for themselves its significance and their role in it.

As this is the last session of the *Mission and Philosophy Retreat*, the conversation takes one further step back and briefly reflects on the whole retreat. This allows participants to process what has happened to them as individuals and as a group, as well as to focus on the implications of their work for their organization.

The *Mission and Philosophy Retreat* can be and has been modified and adapted to meet a variety of needs. It is useful to new organizations, divisions or teams, as they formulate their task. It is useful among older organizations that find the need to rearticulate or recreate their existing mission and philosophy. The key to this process is the participation of as many people in the organization as possible in helping to shape and therefore, to own the corporate mission and philosophy. Although in most cases participants in the *Mission and Philosophy Retreat* are senior executives, the process of communicating the work of this retreat is critical and is most effective when done in a participative mode, enabling the broader membership to internalize the corporate mission and philosophy.

In the words of David Hurst, ''. . . Leadership is really a process, an ongoing dynamic relationship among a number of individuals in search of meaning. If leadership is effective, then these individuals will develop a shared vision, a sense of common purpose, and the ability to make their own unique contributions. Their work will satisfy their need for both identity and community, their striving both to become what they are and, at the same time, to belong to something larger than themselves. . . . 'When the great leader has done his work, the people will say ''We did it ourselves,'' ' wrote Lao Tzu in the fifth century B.C.''

PART FOUR

Benefits of the *Technology of Participation*

CHAPTER 10

Enhanced Individual Productivity

Organizations that have employed the *Technology of Participation (ToP)* benefit from **enhanced individual productivity, improved organizational effectiveness** and **heightened corporate competitiveness.**

ToP enhances the productivity of individuals within an organization by giving them a sense of ownership. This generates the commitment to see that the job gets done and the motivation to see that it gets done well. Ownership creates a sense of responsibility that allows people to take charge, make decisions and take risks in order to ensure that the plan they created is implemented.

Let's take a closer look at how *ToP* fosters those qualities that are key to productivity: **commitment, motivation** and **responsibility.**

Commitment: The Power Behind Performance

Warren Bennis and Burt Nanus report in their book, *Leaders,* that the "Public Agenda Forum undertook a major survey of the American nonmanagerial workforce not long ago, with the following disturbing results:

- Fewer than 1 out of every 4 job holders say that they are currently working at full potential.
- One half said they do not put effort into their job over and above what is required to hold onto it.
- The overwhelming majority, 75 percent, said that they could be significantly more effective than they presently are.

- Close to 6 out of 10 Americans on the job believe that they 'do not work as hard as they used to.'

"Even more troubling is the possibility that the tendency to withhold effort from the job may be increasing," Bennis and Nanus say. "A number of observers pointed out that a considerable gap exists between the number of hours people are paid for working and the number of hours spent in productive labor. There is evidence that this gap is widening. A University of Michigan survey shows the difference between paid hours and actual working hours grew by 10 percent during the seventies."

Bennis and Nanus conclude that "people talk about the decline of the work ethic. . . . But what there really is is a commitment gap. Leaders have failed to instill vision, meaning and trust in their followers. They have failed to empower them."

"People want to make a commitment to a purpose, a goal, a vision that is bigger than themselves," write Naisbitt and Aburdene. "One of the best-kept secrets in America is that people are aching to make a commitment—if they only had the freedom and environment in which to do so."

Karen Carpenter of the Minnesota Energy Agency tells a story of how such commitment is built with *ToP*:

"The Energy Agency started during the oil embargo and was the favorite child of all the Governors. It had started out as a board of some five people and had grown to an agency of 150 full-time staff. . . .

"Just a month before the fiscal crisis hit in 1980, the legislature passed a grant of $1.25 million for our program. We were really excited because we'd be able to draft a first-of-its-kind model for community energy planning. We had some $70,000 to hire consultants to help write this great document that would be the 'Bible' on the subject. . . .

"But after the crisis the first thing the Governor did, naturally, was look for large pieces of money that had just been approved that he could zap. And our grants were the first to go. So we figured 'we don't have any money to give to communities, but we still have us, so we'll just go on with this book and find a way without money.' But as time wore on we discovered we were going to lose five of the twelve members of our group. . . .

"While I was trying to figure out how I would rally this group, half of whom were going to be laid off, for another nine months, I was introduced to the ICA. We decided to do a two-and-a-half day group session to plan how we would complete the book project in spite of staff and budget cuts.

"I was used to a more traditional planning process. . . . I was very nervous about the whole thing. We had such divergent personalities . . . I thought this could turn into a war—despite assurances from the facilitators that it would work out just wonderfully.

"What it did was sort of tilt everybody on their ear. It made people think differently. That's exactly what the facilitators told me it would do, because the process starts with the vision. We'd always started with listing our problems, and five hours later everybody

142

would be groaning 'Oh my gosh.' So when we started by asking what we want to see in the future, what our vision is for our project, people were really surprised. . . .

"When we were folding up things and closing the meeting, the most cynical guy I have ever known was standing and smiling, singing a song with everybody. We were so high. We wrote a story about ourselves and named it 'The Little Activity That Could.' It was the story of our organization, and we were crying when we wrote it. It was sad and yet for the time being everyone was still on board and we had just charted our future. At that point I felt that the happy ending in the story could be true, that we could conquer the world. . . .

"We kept right on working," Carpenter continued. "We went on and continued the work for the next nine months, although we were sad because most of the people who were getting laid off hadn't found other jobs.

"The most amazing thing was that for some time after the official layoff date the people that were laid off drifted back in to finish the work that was undone! It was incredible. They came without pay. They were that committed to it.

"Everything that we planned on getting done, got done. The book got done. It is still a model and someday when we have another energy crisis, it will get pulled out. It was so good."

Participation is perhaps the surest way to inspire commitment. Participation in planning and decision-making leads to ownership, and that in turn builds the commitment that is a prerequisite for excellence in workmanship.

"Ownership is a psychological condition, not merely a legal one," explains Lawrence M. Miller. "Ownership is the condition in which the individual feels that his or her own well-being is tied to that of the organization. It is the condition in which the individual is willing to sacrifice immediate self-gain for the good of the whole, in which the employee believes in the interdependency between the self and the organization. The individual will protect the organization from harm as he would protect his home, family, or community. When the psychology of ownership is present, the employee experiences pleasure if the firm succeeds and suffers pain if it fails. This is the unity we should be seeking."

"What are the keys to creating this unity?" Miller asks. He replies that two of the most important are to "give the greatest possible responsibility to the lowest possible levels of the company," and that "the greatest degree of involvement and consensus should be sought from all levels."

Leadership: Motivation Through Shared Responsibility

This downstream flow of responsibility is precisely what *ToP* accomplishes. It involves workers in the planning process and includes their ideas in the group's consensus. Workers who contribute their input to a plan feel pride of ownership. They become committed to the plan's success and see themselves as integral to its execution. They helped to draw it up; now they feel responsible for carrying it out.

Peter Drucker writes, "the employee on all levels from the lowest to the highest needs to be given genuine responsibility. . . . He must be held responsible for setting the goals for his own work and for managing himself by objectives and self-control. He must be held responsible for the constant improvement of the entire operation—what the Japanese call 'continuous learning.' He must share responsibly in thinking through and setting the enterprise's goals and objectives, and in making the enterprise's decisions. This is not 'democracy'; it is citizenship."

Jack Sheehan, the Chicago area director of the Economic Development Office at Illinois Bell, assists many local development groups that have used the *ToP Strategic Planning Process* through a grant from Chicago's Department of Economic Development. "I think the most important thing is that the groups have actually done what they agreed to do at these meetings," Sheehan said. "Before, we had planning meetings and people would talk for hours and go away saying, 'Now what's going to happen?' When we are finished with [ToP] meetings, we say, 'Okay, you agreed you would do this and it's going to be done by next Wednesday,' and it gets done."

Such spreading of responsibility is particularly helpful for companies undergoing change. Managing change effectively requires that people "buy in" to changes that are occurring by participating in shaping the transition. Rosabeth Moss Kanter and Barry A. Stein wrote of "the need to involve your own people in adapting to the new idea or model. Change of any sort, we've come to understand, is threatening when it's done to you, but an opportunity when it's done by you. This act of customizing builds ownership. People 'buy in' because they help create the change. They are actively involved, rather than passive recipients of something their boss is making them do."

> Química Flesch, a small chemical manufacturing firm in Chile, had for many years been a family-owned concern. But it sold 50% of its shares to the Sun Chemical Company of New York in the early 1980's to gain access to broader markets.
>
> The change created an identity crisis for the managers and employees. They were now a very small unit of a very large corporation. Managers and employees felt that their own style and culture, developed as a family-owned company, was threatened through the new relationship with a head office of a multinational corporation thousands of miles away. Productivity slumped.
>
> The general manager, Carlos Schlessinger, decided to enlist his whole workforce to help revive flagging morale and productivity. He engaged *ToP* facilitators to lead a *Strategic Planning Session* for all 70 employees.
>
> Several months later, the facilitators paid a follow-up visit. After a few minutes of trying to explain everything that had happened since the seminar, Schlesinger decided it would be simpler just to take them on a tour of the plant.
>
> The first thing the visitors noticed was dramatically improved landscaping with much more greenery. Next, they saw a new employee dining room, and noted that the working areas

were far neater and tidier. Schlesinger pointed out that the walls had been freshly painted by workers volunteering on their own time. He said that the next meeting with the Sun Chemical people was going to be held in the factory because he and the workers were so proud of its new look. The laboratory also was completely renovated and sparkling clean, new procedures manuals had been published, and new job description manuals had been written by the workers themselves.

The union leader reported that there was a new feeling of trust between management and workers. She said that workers now felt that they could tell managers about problems, and managers were no longer afraid to criticize the workers. Before the seminar, managers and workers had all held back for fear of causing resentment. She noted that now the managers often ate in the workers' cafeteria, for example, allowing for casual mingling and good will to develop.

The union head also mentioned a proposal from the seminar that the company provide summer homes for the workers at a nearby beach (it is a common practice in Chile for companies to provide housing for their employees). Management had subsequently discussed the proposal with workers and suggested that by deferring some of their current benefits, the workers could use the money that was saved to finance those homes, and actually own them. This had been a terrific shot in the arm for worker morale. It indicated to them that management's faith in their abilities was higher than ever.

Most impressive, however, was that the firm's sales increased by 40% in the six months following the seminar! Some of that increase could be attributed to changes in the Chilean economy, but Schlessinger said most of it could be traced directly to changes effected by the *ToP Strategic Planning Session*.

"Even our clients notice the difference," he smiled. "They keep saying 'Something is different here.'"

As they begin to feel that they and their ideas really make a difference to the company, passive workers become actively engaged in the creative change process. Eventually employees begin to feel a sense of ownership not only of a set of plans, but of the corporation itself. Ownership builds loyalty and morale by generating a vested interest in the company's success and well-being.

"The successful manager of the future will make full use of the collective wisdom of those within his jurisdiction," Miller asserts, "and he will learn to derive pleasure, not from the making of decisions, but from assuring that the best possible decision is made."

Michael Maccoby of Harvard makes the point that "good leadership at the top is not good enough." Maccoby explains that for "companies and government bureaucracies to function effectively, inter-dependent teams at different levels need leaders," too. A participative environment creates that leadership, along with a healthy new attitude of self-management.

"We continually emphasize local control for local problems, because it's simply not possible to figure it all out from the top," observed Ray Stata, President and Chairman of Analog Devices Inc. "The management hierarchy needs to provide direction, awareness, and sense of how the game is played, but it needs to respect the greater ability of small groups to solve their own problems.''

Miller adds that ''people who get into difficulties can, in most cases, get out of them. By doing so, they enhance their skills and confidence, and are less likely to get into similar situations in the future. Most problem solvers sent to help depart with their 'silver bullets,' leaving the local folks just as incapable as when they arrived. Problem solvers must involve the person or group that owns the problems in solving it, and leave them with the skills and confidence to solve their own difficulties and to make future decisions on their own.''

The National Rice Producers Committee of Peru, an association of local rice producers' committees, is funded by assessments on each kilo of rice sold to the government owned rice marketing company. The funds are applied to technical assistance and services for the rice growers.

Recently the committee experienced political interference as activists from many different parties infiltrated the local committees. The national leaders were alerted because they wanted to keep the committees non-political to safeguard their unity. They resolved to develop a strong sense of identity to strengthen unity and to guarantee better service for all members, regardless of political affiliation.

ToP was applied in a *Strategic Planning Session* for the National Committee. Perhaps the most important impact of the session was the realization that, although they are not a commercial company, the National Rice Producers Committee is the fourth largest economic force in Peru, based on the combined income of the producers. That realization gave the producers a sense of identity, pride, and responsibility. They determined to use their power wisely to benefit their members and not to let it be usurped by political activists.

Out of the seminar came four proposals geared ''toward the massive mobilization of 6,000 rice producers.'' These included 1) regional planning sessions to develop a broad base of support for the committee, 2) increased communications between the rice producers and the committee, 3) leadership development and 4) management training for the rice growers. The planning seminar was immediately followed by a four day program that trained 25 local leaders from the coastal and remote jungle regions in techniques for corporate planning and implementation.

One result reported to date has been consolidation of several small but active local committees into one regional committee. This move increased the strength of the organization as well as the power of the rice producers as a unified body.

Recently, the Committee has decided to assign 10% of its resources to Research and Technology Transfer, which includes leadership training.

These are just a few illustrations of the many organizations that have found that the sense of ownership in an organization and its future provided by *ToP* methods generates the commitment, motivation and responsibility that result in enhanced individual productivity. The following chapters illustrate how *ToP* generates **improved organizational effectiveness** and **heightened corporate creativity**.

CHAPTER 11

Improved Organizational Effectiveness

Participation creates **alignment** within an organization as members help to shape, and therefore commonly own the shared vision of their organization. This alignment brings about a sense of unity and **cooperation**, resulting in new levels of **trust** and **teamwork**. **Communication** is enhanced within and between departments and levels of the organization, thus creating the conditions in which **creativity** flourishes. All of this results in **improved organizational effectiveness**.

Alignment: Developing a Shared Vision

"When the diverse elements of the organization are aligned, the energy is focused and the capacity for concerted action improved," write Buckley and Steffy. "Priorities become clear, and the contributions of each employee are maximized. As leaders learn that creating the passion and commitment of aligned action is the 'stuff' of management, the awesome power of many would-be champions and inspiring visionaries within the organization will be unleashed."

The key to alignment is a shared vision, acting like a magnet that pulls all the units together toward the same direction. Kiefer and Senge say that alignment brings "the realization within each individual of the extraordinary power of a group committed to a common vision." In such organizations "people do not assume they are powerless. They believe deeply in the power of visioning, the power of the individual to determine his or her own destiny."

Detroit's Mount Carmel Mercy Hospital was attempting to maintain its urban commitment while opening up suburban satellites and to maintain quality services despite the

147

prospect of limited funding. At a three day retreat, 95 staff members drew up a vision of the future and an action plan for all 2200 employees to carry out.

Among the accomplishments of the hospital's task forces were: 1) becoming one of the first hospitals to successfully adopt federal reimbursement regulations for Medicare patients; 2) purchasing new equipment to keep up with the revolution in medical technology; 3) initiating ''Golden Pond'' lectures and other innovative services for senior citizens; 4) developing a brochure for doctors to give to patients to better explain the hospital and its services; 5) holding numerous school presentations on health topics; and 6) instituting an ethic of friendliness and hospitality toward both patients and staff, symbolized by a uniformed doorman stationed at the entrance to welcome entering patients and visitors.

''In the two years since the *Strategic Planning Session,*'' reported hospital spokesman George Hazler, ''we have turned much of our practical vision into reality. While we can't say we've achieved all our goals, we've established a precedent for success through participation, and have demonstrated what we can do when our creativity and energy is focused on our organization's future.''

Cooperation: Tearing Down the Walls of Isolation

''The new corporate leader will succeed by creating unity among persons in the organization and between the organization and its members,'' writes Miller. ''A spirit of oneness, harmony of purpose, common interests, and action will characterize the most successful organizations. All management practices will be aimed at the creation of this harmony and productivity and performance in our organizations will be improved as we create a spirit of unity between people at all levels.''

This quality of cooperation was also developed at Colorado's Copper Mountain Ski Resort which found itself embroiled in the fiercely competitive ''ski wars'' among Colorado resorts.

Andy Daly, Copper Mountain's CEO at the time, had identified ''excellent and consistent customer service'' as the marketing edge Copper Mountain needed to achieve if it was to survive. He asked Marty Seldman, a private consultant who uses *ToP* methods in his work, to facilitate a planning session with his 13 top people to develop a comprehensive plan to anticipate and provide for everything a customer could want.

The result of the planning session was a plan so comprehensive that it nearly overwhelmed Daly. He was somewhat skeptical about getting it implemented because it was so big and complex and because his staff tended to be strong-willed and individualistic. To pull off this plan, they would have to work together more closely than he had ever seen them do before.

A major component of the plan was a program to train the 1100 member staff in customer service skills. By the 90-day follow-up session, the training program was developed. By the opening of the ski season, all 1100 staff had been trained. The other components of the plan were also implemented on schedule. The staff were even using the *ToP* methods they learned from Seldman in ongoing problem solving as a way of gathering information from different perspectives and as a way to encourage cooperation rather than competition.

Daly was delighted. He said he had never seen so much hard work and commitment from his staff before, let alone the timely completion of a plan. He attributed it to the group's participation in building the plan and the sharing of the vision with all the workers through the training program.

Daly was not the only one who was pleased. The staff had discovered a new team spirit. Management had a new image of the staff and had gained respect for their creativity and commitment. Finally, and most important, feedback from customers was enthusiastic.

One key factor in cooperation is trust—among individuals and between workers and management. *ToP* methods enable workers and managers to appreciate each other's situations, struggles and abilities. Isolation and antagonism are gradually eliminated. Once those divisive walls are torn down, they are replaced by a new spirit of trust and cooperation.

A conference of citizens and educators in Appleton, Wisconsin, helped break down the rigid and somewhat unfair stereotypes each group held of the other.

In 1985 Wisconsin Governor Tony Earl signed into law a bill called the Education for Employment Act. Responding to complaints from local businesses that the newly hired employees hadn't been properly prepared by local schools, the act mandated that all of the state's 432 school districts must have an Education for Employment plan in place no later than March 1988 (this has since been changed to 1991).

The Appleton school district resolved to hold a "Partnership Conference" for business leaders and educators to draw up a plan for an Education for Employment program for their district. They called upon ICA staff to facilitate their conference.

The conference theme was "Building the Workforce for the Year 2001" and the ratio of educators to business people was about 1:1. A second conference, "Partnership Conference II" was held one year later.

Results of the conference were far reaching—extending all the way to children in the schools who would some day constitute the workforce. Companies prepared brochures about their activities. They conducted tours for busloads of school children. Local restaurants hosted luncheons where students, parents, business people and educators talked over the problems of each school. Teachers spent part of their summer vacations "shadowing" a local businessperson to observe and even pitch in, acquiring some "hands-on" experience regarding what happens during a normal workday. Teachers thereby developed exercises about work attitudes and basic skills for inclusion in their lesson plans. Business people began to shadow teachers in classrooms observing techniques and curriculum. An "Inventions Convention" was held at one elementary school, encouraging students to create a product that performs a task. Another elementary school set up a 2-day "Career Fest," with business and industry representatives presenting mini lectures one day and a display of products and services a week later. Pleased with the results of the first two conferences, the schools and businesses of Appleton have made them annual events.

Appleton's plan has become the prototype for Wisconsin schools. Besides preparing students for future careers, the joint activities built new bridges of communication between the business and education communities. The two groups finally understood each other. "We had no idea how professional and skilled our teachers are," the business people explained. Educators commented, "We learned that the business people really care about the community."

Cooperation and trust mean less infighting and back-stabbing, as everyone seeks to achieve the same end, rather than to protect their individual turf. Through *ToP* methods, wasteful competition is replaced by cooperation.

In an October, 1986 article in *Savvy,* Rosabeth Moss Kanter debunked the trend she calls "cowboy management," that actually "makes a virtue out of competition. . . . When internal competition is fostered within a company—when several players are doing the same thing in pursuit of a single prize—the result is a waste of resources that few companies can afford. Consciously creating winners and losers is simply bad strategy; an organization needs everyone's best efforts, which usually means everyone's cooperation. . . . In every high-performing company I've seen—in my own research and consulting practice as well as in that of other researchers—cooperation was more effective than competition in fostering productivity and innovation."

Communication and Teamwork: Built on Trust

The cooperation and trust that result from alignment around a common vision help to unblock the channels of communication within an organization. The result is greater creativity.

John H. Zenger wrote in *Training* Magazine about the attitude managers often take toward communication: "Some curtail it. They communicate only on a 'need-to-know' basis. Managers are inclined to stay in their offices. Communication, they complain, takes too much time. For many, information is power to be hoarded, not something to be shared. And indeed, those perceptions have some validity—if you define your role as one of control and administration, not leadership."

But William H. Peace warned, in the *Harvard Business Review,* what can happen when managers follow the traditional way of keeping their cards close to the chest. Recalling his experience as general manager of a Westinghouse division, Peace said, "Although my staff and I had our goals, tasks, and priorties well defined, large parts of the organization didn't know what was going on." The result was that "employees and managers often assumed the worst about one another and acted accordingly. And as suspicion built on itself, the organization's goals took a backseat to turf and survival. Quality, productivity, and customer satisfaction meant very little."

The Pas Lumber Company in Prince George, British Columbia also had difficulties with trust and communication, although they hadn't yet perceived the problem that way.

A year before their *ToP Strategic Planning Seminar,* The Pas had fitted their sawmill with state-of-the-art technology, designed to get as much wood product as possible out of every tree. Laser guided and computer directed, it was perhaps the most advanced sawmill in the nation. They now sought to determine how they might produce at a rate equal to design capacity, while completing the transition to high tech. That transition meant retraining the workers who remained after many had been displaced by new technology.

The *Strategic Planning Session* with 13 top managers started with discussions on production costs, but during the session it surfaced that some employees resisted the new technology because they were afraid that eventually it would cost them their jobs. Those misgivings retarded the training needed to push the plant up to full production.

Although The Pas generally had high marks in the area of human relations, with fair and enlightened management practices, many of the strategic directions evolving from the sessions were focused on employee-management relationships. The almost complete lack of communication within and between departments was also tackled by the group. For instance, some office people had never set foot inside the sawmill. And the people in the planing mill never spoke to the people at the sawmill. President Don Gould later observed that "there existed poor communications within divisions as well as between divisions. These factors had a detrimental effect on the productivity coming from the start-up of the new computerized sawmill. . . . The session was the first time that representatives of various divisions of The Pas were assembled to discuss joint views on various questions facing the company."

Follow-up included a seminar to teach supervisors how to relate to their employees and a safety seminar with 60 managers and union leaders. The 12 hour safety session inspired a great feeling of camaraderie among supervisors and union reps who shared jokes and beer afterward. They soon also shared in a greatly improved safety record.

Within 90 days after the planning seminar, every strategy on the quarter's implementation calender had been finished and checked off. Sixty percent of those tasks scheduled for later in the year had already been started. President Gould and others noted a distinct attitude change and a very positive reaction to the program.

"The total involvement with the ICA covered an eighteen month period and resulted in many tangible improvements," Gould later commented. "Most of the difficulties resulting from the sawmill modernization have been overcome and there exists today a more harmonious team approach among key players in the various divisions of The Pas Lumber Company."

Charles Kiefer and Peter M. Senge note that leaders in organizations with the capacity to shape their own destinies "typically involve themselves heavily in teaching employees how the organization operates." They quote Tandem Corporation's Jim Treybig as noting that "Each person in the company must understand the essence of the business."

Participation provides this understanding of the "big picture" to all members of an organization. To participate in planning for their department, for example, people need to have an understanding of the overall organization —its operation, its resources, constraints, etc. Such overall understanding tells employees how their department fits into the total picture and the role it plays in the success of the enterprise.

ToP methods help to keep everyone focused on the larger picture rather than on the personalities of group members. Exchanges therefore address not only surface problems, but permit deeply buried issues to be raised without anyone feeling threatened. Because participants set their sights on a common task, rather than on each other, communication is elevated to a level beyond pettiness and pure self-interest.

"You put a group of people in the same room and you have personality differences," noted the executive director of Chicago's Greater Southwest Development Corporation, James Capraro. "Some people don't like other people, or you might have people who are intimidated by meetings and just afraid to speak up, or you have people who are too verbose and might take over the meeting. The techniques of [*ToP*] have ways to take care of all of that."

"What you have," another executive from a major airline told the facilitators, "is a very fine facilitation process to get people to think in a non-threatening environment."

Robert C. Mansfield, the vice president and general manager of McDonald's-Australia, reported that their **Strategic Planning Seminar** resulted in "much more involvement by the mid-management group in contributing their views to top management for consideration. They now feel they can bring up the problems for discussion rather than just putting up with the problems."

The non-confrontational dialogue that starts during the teamwork stage in a *ToP* planning event and then carries on during implementation and follow-up, can eventually become part of the firm's ongoing culture. Many of today's leading management experts believe that such a culture is a distinguishing trait of a top-notch company.

Peters and Waterman note that "the task force is an exciting, fluid, ad hoc device in the excellent companies. It is virtually the way of solving and managing thorny problems, and an unparalled spur to practical action."

The flexibility inherent in small teams or ad hoc task forces lets organizations quickly respond to change. And a participative environment is the atmosphere in which they perform most effectively.

Russ Goodman, an officer of the Department of Human Services of the State of Minnesota, tells the story of the team building taking place within his organization.

> "We have a fairly large department . . . very big and very diversified. It serves everything from people who just can't find a job to unwed mothers, to very seriously disabled, retarded people. . . .

> "The Governor's office had asked for a 20-year tactical plan from each department. [We engaged the *Technology of Participation*.] After initial interviews with the commissioner and assistant commissioner a two-day Design Conference was held to determine the focus question. The question we arrived at was, 'What would we do if client self-sufficiency was

our mission? How would we go about achieving that?' We went through a standard *Strategic Planning Session* involving 120 staff to look at that question.

"Programs or aspects of programs can become so specialized that you can have people with very compatible missions unaware of what each other is doing," explained Goodman in describing one of the department's contradictions. "It's inevitable that policy conflicts develop out of very positive motivation to do the best job.

"From our tactics chart we selected about sixteen different items to work on. One of our tactics was cross-bureau teams representing the various departments and bureaus. The proposal was to work in cross-bureau teams when a program or policy has a significant effect on clients, if it is controversial or if it represents a significant change in what the department is doing."

Goodman reports that the more effective teamwork and coordination between the bureaus set the stage for innovative thinking. "The idea occurred in the planning process originally and then we did, in fact, have teams that worked for a good 90 days on those issues, and every single team completed their work and submitted a report with recommendations.

"In addition to better teamwork and innovative thinking," Goodman said, "something else happened. Ideas opened up and changed. Things started getting carried through. You can count things now. It was like the transformation of a culture."

The **improved organizational effectiveness** that comes from alignment, cooperation and enhanced communication and teamwork does not just benefit the internal operations and morale of an organization. It also leads to **heightened corporate competitiveness**.

CHAPTER 12

Heightened Corporate Competitiveness

In order to stay competitive in today's fast-changing environment, organizations of all kinds must foster creative thinking. More important, they must be able to translate that **creativity** into **innovative approaches** to developing products and services, as well as internal operating modes. Finally, they must have the capacity for realistic **implementation** of these innovative approaches.

Creativity: The Competitive Edge

In *Re-inventing the Corporation* John Naisbitt and Patricia Aburdene wrote, "In the new information-rich, decentralized, global society, creativity will be increasingly valued in business. Creativity is the corporation's competitive edge.

"The need for creativity in the re-invented corporation is a relatively new phenomenon," they go on to say. After all, "the mass production-oriented industrial society relied on uniformity to produce results." But they report that "in the new corporation, creativity and individuality are organizational treasures."

Companies that employ *ToP* methods are seldom at a loss for such ideas. Rather, they are often in step with the trend observed by Perry Pascarella, the executive editor of *Industry Week.* In his book *The New Achievers,* he noted that "Management is heading toward a new state of mind—a new perception of its own role and that of the organization. It is slowly moving from seeking power to empowering others, from controlling people to enabling them to be creative. . . ."

One way that executives make this happen is by creating a climate of intense informal communication. As a senior manager at Hewlett Packard told Peters and Waterman, "We're not really sure how the innovative process works. But there's one thing we do know: the easy communications, the absence of barriers to talking to one another are essential.'' Increased communication is one of the major payoffs of using *ToP* methods.

Particularly important in the creative process are communications across a variety of departments and disciplines. Rosabeth Moss Kanter discussed her study of a group of innovative managers. "The most common roadblock they had to overcome in their accomplishment, if they faced any at all, was poor communication with other departments on whom they depended for information; at the same time, more than a quarter of them were directly aided by cooperation from departments other than their own as a critical part of their innovation."

By bringing out a diverse range of perspectives within the framework of a focused context, participation produces an immediate upsurge in creativity. Kanter noted that "innovating companies seem to deliberately create a 'marketplace of ideas,' recognizing that a multiplicity of points of view need to be brought to bear on a problem. It is not the 'caution of committees' that is sought—reducing risk by spreading responsibility—but the better idea that comes from a clash and an integration of perspectives." The *ToP methods* bring those diverse perspectives together, resulting in a spontaneous combustion of creativity.

The *Technology of Participation* has demonstrated repeatedly that it sets up an environment where such creativity can flourish. An executive of a major airline reported that "there's a creative synergy, an awful lot of thought enhancement that comes from that group effort. One person comes up with an idea, and I see it on the board and my mind starts working, and then I jump on it, and one idea is built on top of another. You can just see the wheels turning as a result of the conversation, as you sit across from one another, talking and sharing ideas. That fertilization, or cross-fertilization, of ideas, is very evident when you go through the process.''

Innovation: Doing New Things New Ways

"The trouble with much of the advice business gets today about the need to be more vigorously creative is that its advocates often fail to distinguish between creativity and innovation,'' observed Harvard's Theodore Leavitt. "Creativity is thinking up new things. Innovation is doing new things.... A powerful new idea can kick around unused in a company for years, not because its merits are not recognized, but because nobody has assumed the responsibility for converting it from words into action. Ideas are useless unless used. The proof of their value is only in their implementation.''

Managers often look upon creativity and innovativeness as something rare, something that they might be lucky enough to stumble across in a few of their brightest employees. They figure that when they find those qualities, the thing to do is guard them, coddle them and hope they'll bring the company great profits.

In participative environments, however, managers don't just hope to find those qualities. They actively create climates in which creativity and innovation can grow. That way, everyone in the organization has the opportunity to discover and refine their own creative talents.

As management consultant Cass Bettinger wrote in *The American Banker,* "innovation does not just happen in corporations but is the result of a corporate culture that has created an environment which supports innovative thinking."

It's not surprising that Naisbitt and Aburdene report that "*Fortune* magazine's eight most innovative companies in America . . . are masters of the cross-disciplinary team." They quote *Fortune's* Stratford P. Sherman, who wrote that at those companies "people in different disciplines are simply not allowed to remain in isolation. Business units are kept small in part to throw engineers, marketers, and finance experts together into the sort of tight groups most often found in start-up companies." Those groups are also, of course, very similar to the cross-departmental task forces that are formed in *ToP* sessions.

One well-known company that reaped the benefits of innovative thinking and action is The Bay. This chain of department stores is one of Canada's two largest retailers. It evolved from the legendary Hudson Bay Company.

> In 1983 manager Alan Herbert was temporarily transferred from the Human Resources Department at The Bay's Toronto office to a line management function in the Data Processing section. He was given nine months to set in place a new credit card system. The entire department, consisting of 36 people, was then to be shut down. Herbert's orders were only to convert to a new system and maintain the normal flow of customer billings. But he also resolved to accomplish that assignment without laying anyone off.

> Applying his training in *ToP* methods, Herbert engineered a highly successful transition. He and his staff not only held group meetings to make sure that the group's objectives were clear and well understood and to gather input about system bottlenecks—they also planned some truly innovative moves.

> The most important of these was a shift in the work schedule from a five day to a six day week, and from three 12-hour to five eight-hour shifts. At the same time, jobs were rotated so that all employees could learn skills to enable them to work in other departments.

> In addition to installing a more efficient billing system, with new ways to eliminate or streamline record keeping, every section employee, except one who refused to accept any of the transfer or rescheduling options, was kept on board by the company.

Innovative thinking by Herbert and his team gave loyalty and morale a very big boost at The Bay.

Mercy Hospital and Medical Center of Chicago also found the *Technology of Participation* to be a springboard for innovative approaches. The current crisis in insurance coverage has many American hospitals scrambling to cut costs. Marketing mechanisms, consequently, are being created across the industry to combat declining business.

> In 1984 Mercy Hospital experienced a 4% drop in occupancy rate and chose a *ToP Strategic Planning Session* to help them map out an appropriate response.

The first step toward establishing a participative environment was the formation of a Marketing Steering Committee of administrators and doctors. The free flow of communication that resulted yielded a number of hard-hitting but on-target innovations.

Empty beds were reallocated to busier departments, a move that expanded the Alcohol Treatment Unit, the Geriatric Unit and the Outpatient Surgery Unit. It also averted potential layoffs. New facilities and an option to rent space to start a satellite center were secured. An Immediate Care Center was opened and aggressively marketed. A fund raiser and a sales person were hired and a $15 million fund raising drive called "For the Sake of Mercy" was launched. Health fairs were conducted at churches in nearby communities to attract new clients. New public aid and HMO contracts were negotiated, and a campaign was initiated to instruct industries on how to set up preventive health programs. Staff members made presentations about Mercy to national and state associations.

These are only a few examples of the innovations created and implemented by the Mercy team. Doctors and staff members at all levels resolved to think in terms of marketing the benefits of their expanded program. Today Mercy Hospital is in very stable financial condition, while maintaining its long-standing tradition of quality service.

Implementation: Getting Plans Off the Shelf and Into Action

"A major consequence of participative planning," wrote the author of *Creating the Corporate Future,* Russell L. Ackoff, "is a reduction of the difficulties normally associated with implementation of plans. People are more inclined to implement plans they have had a hand in producing than those that are handed down to or imposed on them. Through participation, implementation becomes an integral part of the planning process."

That benefit of participation is particularly significant, given the results of recent management surveys. In his book *The Supermanagers,* Robert Heller cited a study by consultant Richard G. Allen of strategic planning practices at 145 leading U.S. companies. Allen reported that the most glaring weakness was implementation. He rated as "very weak" the "degree of implementation and impact of strategy" and "toughness of operating plans to execute strategy." Rated as "extremely weak" was "organization for effective strategy implementation."

These results coincide with those reported by Daniel H. Gray in the *Harvard Business Review.* Gray said that of the companies responding to his survey, "87% reported feelings of disappointment and frustration with their systems" of strategic planning, and of that total, "59% attribute their discontent mainly to difficulties encountered in the implementation of plans."

With the *Technology of Participation,* however, accountability is built in and implementation virtually guaranteed. Since the *ToP Strategic Planning Process* includes task assignments, accountability checks and a detailed calendar for implementation, the process doesn't end when the plan is completed. It moves right from planning into action, assuring that the ideas will be implemented. It also provides for regular reviews for needed mid-course corrections. This allows for team input whenever a strategic direction gets "stuck," and ensures that nothing vital is overlooked.

Since the 90 day clock of the implementation calendar usually begins to run the first day or week after the session is held, the team kicks out of the starting blocks as fast as possible, generating immediate, tangible results that keep their momentum in high gear. Similar accountability measures are built into all ToP planning applications.

Even more important in generating and maintaining momentum is the fact that "planners" and "implementers" are generally the same people. Participants who have created a plan naturally have a personal stake in seeing that "their" plan succeeds. As Heller cautioned: "Separate the responsibility for deciding policy from that for its execution, and you open up a huge gulf into which large parts of the company may inadvertently fall." The *ToP Strategic Planning Process* prevents that gulf from opening up, since the tasks are usually assigned to those attending the session.

Finally, the task assignments give the team members the authority they'll need to act on them, and that's especially important when a task is delicate or unpopular. For example, the strategic plan built by a team of medical and administrative staff at a major hospital called for an employee attitude survey to be conducted within each department. A participant at the planning session was assigned to draw up the questionnaire, distribute it to department heads and collect the completed questionnaires. Not surprisingly, she met with a barrage of complaints when she delivered the questionnaires and asked to have them returned within three days. "Nearly every department head complained about having too much paper work and not enough time," she recounted. "But I reminded them that the survey wasn't my idea. They were at the planning session when we decided to do the survey. They assigned me to organize it. I'm just fulfilling the assignment they gave me. This helped them remember the bigger plan of which the survey was a piece, and they were willing to move on it."

> In Japan, the Yuyasu family department store is part of the Nichii chain of franchised family-owned companies, the third largest such chain in Japan. The Yuyasu store had dominated its market for 100 years. But new competition and social trends have eroded its position until it had the worst sales performance in Nichii's northern region. Nichii assigned a new manager from its central staff to revive the store's sales, polish up its identity, set new directions and spur the motivation of 100 employees. The manager was also instructed to wipe out the store's accumulated debt. All of this was to be accomplished within 2 or 3 years. The manager chose the *Technology of Participation* to help him meet the challenge.

> The Japanese consensus process usually requires much discussion over an extended period of time, but a *ToP Strategic Planning Session* enabled them to find the needed new directions quickly. Soon after the meeting there was a great flurry of activity. A new cleanup plan was implemented and six truckloads of debris were hauled away. Two months later when the facilitators visited, the store was completely cleaned up; they could hardly recognize the place.

Three months after the *ToP Strategic Planning Session* with Nichii, managers who had participated in it were the assistant facilitators for a one-day planning session with all 100 employees, including part time workers. The theme of the session was "Making our shops attractive and our service enticing."

Sales increased quickly; soon average monthly sales shot up by 112% and their store vaulted from thirty–seventh place to fifth place in regional sales. Within two and a half years the Yuyasu store netted a profit of 140,000,000 yen ($700,000) wiping out a long standing debt of 96 million yen ($480,000). Yuyasu now had working capital for expansion.

The Nichii manager said that the **ToP Strategic Planning Session**:

- helped him get strategic information quickly as he began his new job in a difficult situation;

- gave each manager a sense of responsibility and permission to act in an interdependent manner toward a common goal;

- revitalized the workplace and brought about consciousness of the importance of cooperation;

- helped them deal flexibly with society's changing needs;

- catalyzed a "personal consciousness revolution" and turned peoples' eyes toward their life purpose; and

- motivated people and built teams that were immediately effective, resulting in a dramatic increase in sales within a short period of time;

Under a contract with the City of Chicago's Department of Economic Development, *ToP Strategic Planning* and *ToP Leadership Training* have been applied with the Department's 100 delegate agencies, including chambers of commerce, local development associations, and local business associations.

> "The ICA has been uniformly successful . . . with all the groups, irrespective of geographical area of the city, background, or level of development," noted the Department's Deputy Commissioner, Art Vazquez. "A good example is the Industrial Council of Northwest Chicago. They were very resistant, first of all, in accepting the training offered, but once they had the experience of coming together and having a three-hour workshop, they insisted that the ICA return and do another three hour workshop and then another one, and the result of that was a very sound detailed strategic plan that continues to be the model of development for their area."

Speaking at the "Chicago Works Together" Citizens Conference, in which *ToP* methods were applied, the late Harold Washington, then Mayor of Chicago, referred to that neighborhood development process when he said:

> "For the first time in the city's history, specific development goals and policies have been articulated. City goals and policies are now taken out of the dimly lit backrooms and placed in the light of public scrutiny, the public scrutiny of people like yourselves who

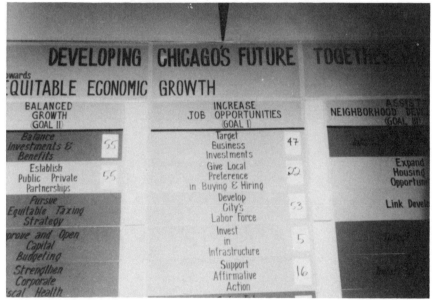

have the desire and the techniques to make them even better. It is a plan that has been used widely and woven into the very fabric of our city's operation. It is a process, not a product, and it's a process because we feel it is like democracy in a sense, that it goes on and on and on and on, constantly improving, constantly weaving, constantly growing, constantly developing and constantly bringing within its orbit those who have something to offer.''

The creativity, innovation and capacity for implementation that are sparked by the use of *ToP* methods in a wide variety of applications help organizations stay on the edge of today's rapidly evolving environment.

EPILOGUE

ToP methods are not the leading edge in organizational development or transformation. That edge lies in the creativity, innovativeness, openness and courage of the organization itself. *ToP* methods can and do, however, create a climate that nourishes those qualities necessary for transformation—alignment, leadership, communication, cooperation, commitment, creativity, innovation and implementation. The benefits described in Part IV are not promises. They are results. They have been reported by hundreds of organizations that have applied *ToP* to meet specific objectives.

This book was written at the behest of clients and associates who encouraged us to document these methods. Nevertheless, some have cautioned us about publishing them in such a "how-to" style. They fear that the methods will be diluted or distorted by unskilled or unscrupulous practitioners. Others suggested that we print a disclaimer, stating that unless a facilitator is trained in *ToP* methods by the ICA, we assume no responsibility for the results of their efforts.

No book can substitute for hands-on training, especially for such a people-oriented process as *ToP.* We discourage anyone from trying to conduct a major application such as a *ToP Strategic Planning Session* without first observing and being trained in *ToP* facilitation. However, the methods themselves, as detailed in Part II, are simple and straightforward and we encourage team leaders, department managers and others responsible for overseeing group planning and implementation to put them to use. For further training or to schedule a *ToP* event for your organization, contact the nearest ICA office listed at the back of this book.

Although this book was begun in a year when competition was the watchword, it seems that already a new mode is emerging—that of cooperation or partnership. We see this as a tremendously hopeful sign. The future of this planet demands cooperation and partnership between people, organizations, sectors of society and nations. *ToP* has proven to be highly effective in cross-sector and inter-organizational planning, such as the International Exposition of Rural Development and the Soviet-American Citizens' Summit. We look forward to developing more applications which foster the partnership paradigm that our planet so urgently needs. We invite organizations and individuals to join us in developing those applications for their communities, social institutions or service organizations.

At the same time, we recognize that most people spend most of their waking hours in the workplace. It is there that many skills, attitudes and operating styles are developed, which are then carried over into other areas of activity, such as family, religion, politics and social concerns. By introducing *ToP* methods into the organizations in which people spend their workdays, the skills, attitudes and patterns of cooperation, commitment, individual responsibility, creativity and innovation which are required to ensure a harmonious future for this planet will spill out into the social and political organizations, fertilizing the planetary soil with seeds of the partnerhsip paradigm. This is why we chose to make these methods available to anyone who reads this book. Winning through participation is a win-win proposition for our planet.

Notes

Page

Introduction

11 "companies that survive": Ralph Barra is quoted by Bill Sapporito in "The Revolt Against Working Smarter," *Fortune* July 21, 1986, p. 65.

11 "clear research evidence": Marshall Shashkin, "Participative Management Remains an Ethica Imperative," *Organizational Dynamics* (an AMA Periodicals Review) Spring 1986, p. 71.

Chapter 1

3 *Change is the only constant:* James D. Robinson is quoted by Steven Prokesch in "Remaking the American C.E.O." *New York Times,* January 25 1987, Section 3, pp. 1, 8.

3 *The ability to adapt:* Ibid.

3 *The modern business world:* Regis McKenna, *The Regis Touch* (Reading, Mass.: Addison-Wesley, 1985), p. 4.

3 *The businesses that survive:* Paul Soloman and Thomas Friedman, *Life and Death on the Corporate Battlefield* (New York: Simon & Schuster, 1982).

4 **We have a choice:** Leroy Fahle's remarks are from an untitled videotape produced by Audio Visual Services, Mt. Carmel Mercy Hospital, Detroit, Mich., 1985.

4 Tom Peters, *Thriving on Chaos* (New York: Harper and Row, 1988).

4 "The biggest change": J. E. Newall, President and C.E.O., DuPont Canada, Inc., script of speech delivered to the Toronto Chapter of the Financial Executives Institute, January 14, 1986.

5 "In the past": "3rd World Becomes a Market: Chief Executives Take Notice of Developing Countries," *Chicago Tribune*, November 9, 1986, Section 7, p. 5B.

5 "floating factory": Alonzo L. McDonald, "Of Floating Factories and Mating Dinosaurs. (The Changing Face of Business)," *Harvard Business Review,* November-December, 1986, p. 82.

5 "excellence": Thomas J. Peters and Robert H. Waterman, Jr., *In Search of Excellence* (New York: Harper & Row, 1982).

5 "diversity costs no more": McKenna, *Regis Touch*, pp. 5–6

6 "In an industrial society,": John Naisbitt and Patricia Aburdene, *Reinventing the Corporation* (New York: Warner Books, 1985), p. 19.

6 "today's workforce is younger": Ibid., p. 6.

6 Naisbitt and Aburdene predict: Ibid., p. 16.

6 "We are moving": Ibid., pp. 207–208.

6 A 1983 Public Agenda Foundation study: Daniel Yankelovich and John Immerwahr, *Putting the Work Ethic to Work: a Public Agenda Report on Restoring American's Competitive Vitality* (New York: Public Agenda Foundation, 1983).

7 "intrapreneurship": Gifford Pinchot III, *Intrapreneuring* (New York: Harper & Row, 1985).

8 William P. Anthony, *Participative Management* (Reading, Mass.: Addison-Wesley, 1978), pp. 6–15.

8 "The role of the manager": Ibid., p.10

8 "This system is premised": Alvin Toffler, *Future Shock* (New York: Random House, 1970), p. 138–9.

8 "For the first time": Marshall Shashkin, "A Manager's Guide to Participative Management," a 1982 American Management Association Briefing, (New York: AMA Membership Publications Division), p. 12

8 "not only to hire": Anthony, *Participative Management,* p. 9.

8 "managers do try": Ibid., p. 10.

9 "The consultive approach": Ibid., p. 11

9 who not only works: William H. Whyte, Jr., *The Organization Man* (New York: Simon & Schuster, 1955).

9 "are precisely those": Toffler, *Future Shock,* p. 125.

9 "Corporations that cling": Naibitt and Aburdene, *Reinventing,* p. 4.

9   "are feverishly sought": Toffler, *Future Shock*, p. 140

10   "is intensified by the arrival": Ibid.

10   "companies don't have": Naisbitt and Aburdene, *Reinventing*, p. 84.

10   "Faced by relatively routine": Toffler, *Future Shock, p.* 145.

10   "Postindustrial Revolution": Anthony, *Participative Management*, p. 8.

10   "Information Age": John Naisbitt, *Megatrends* (New York: Warner Books, 1982), p. 15.

10   "Super-industrial Society": Toffler, *Future Shock*, p. 15.

10   "managers actually share": Anthony, *Participative Management*, p. 11.

10   "from the manager as order-giver": Naisbitt and Aburdene, *Reinventing*, p. 52.

10   "The leader can": Michael Maccoby, *The Leader: A New Face for American Management* (New York: Simon & Schuster, 1981) p. 22.

10   "There can no longer": William J. Crockett, "The Emerging World of the Manager." n.p., n.d.

10   "The hierarchical structure": Naisbitt and Aburdene, *Reinventing*, p. 41.

10   "the typical method": Leonard R. Sayles, *Leadership: What Effective Managers Really Do . . . and How They Do It* (New York: McGraw Hill, 1979).

11   "We're not mounting": David Hanson is quoted by Saporito in "Revolt."

11   "It is not a question": Naisbitt and Aburdene, *Reinventing*, p. 15

11   "As people mature": Shashkin, "Manager's Guide," p. 36.

11   "The very structure": Ibid., p. 38.

11   "a lack of personal recognition": "Pressure on the Job" n.p. October 1986.

12   "We used to think": Naisbitt and Aburdene, *Reinventing,* p. 52.

12   "People cannot be supervised": Ibid., p. 84.

12   "the role of top management": Robert H. Hayes, "Why Strategic Planning Goes Awry," New York Times, April 20, 1986, p. 2F.

12   "the leader who solves": Maccoby, *The Leader,* p. 22.

12   "Do managers think": Paul R. Lawrence, "How to Deal With Resistance to Change,' *Harvard Business Review,* January-February, 1969.

12   "a networking style": Naisbitt and Aburdene, *Reinventing*, p. 62.

12   "frequent, thorough, open": William H. Peace, "I Thought I Knew What Good Management Was," *Harvard Business Review,* March-April 1986, p.65.

12   "We have to think": Naisbitt and Aburdene, *Reinventing*, p. 54.

12   "Inside the corporation": Ibid., p. 52.

12   "the leader is ultimately": Peter Senge is quoted by Walter Kiechel III in "Visionary Leadership and Beyond," *Fortune,* July 21, 1986, p. 128.

13   "If we define": John H. Zenger, "Leadership: Management's Better Half," *Training,* December 1985, p. 44.

13   "the goal of a leader": James MacGregor Burns, *Leadership,* (New York: Harper & Row, 1978).

Chapter 2

15   "The story of Hughes Tool is taken from a report prepared by J.R. Whanger of Houston. n.d.

18   "The failure or refusal": Bill Sapporito, "The Revolt Against Working Smarter," *Fortune* July 21, 1986, p. 60.

18   "a management style": Anthony, *Participative Management,* p. 4.

19   "(1) Goals that are": Sashkin, "Ethical Imperative," p. 68.

19   A survey by the U.S. Chamber of Commerce: Maccoby, *The Leaders.*

20   "middle managers failed": Saporito, "Revolt," p. 60.

20   Just because managers share: Anthony, *Participative Management*, pp. 14-15.

20   American business schools: Shashkin, "Manager's Guide'" p. 9.

20   . . . Most managers probably: Ibid., p. 11.

21   "Managers who think": Saporito, "Revolt", p. 59.

21   "if-it-ain't-broke": Ibid., p. 65.

21   "both research and practice": Sashkin, "Manager's Guide," p. 10.

21   "effective application of participative": Ibid., p. 3.

21   "In technology, we expect": Jay Forrester, "A New Corporate Design," *Industrial Management Review*, (Cambridge, Mass. M.I.T.'s Sloan School of Management, Fall 1965) vol. 7 No. 1, quoted by Naisbitt and Aburdene in *Reinventing*, p. 49.

21   "not the workers": Sapporito, "Revolt," p. 59.

22   "Many chief executives": Prokesch, "Remaking the American C.E.O."

22   "it can lower morale": Anthony, *Participative Management*, p. 11.

22   "My staff and I": Peace, "I Thought I Knew," p.63.

22   ". . . the rapid spread": Shashkin, "Manager's Guide," p. 58.

22   "People who propose": Mitchell Lee Marks, "The Question of Quality Circles," *Psychology Today*, March 1986, p. 46.

22   "They treat symptoms": Ibid., p. 38.

23   "does not go far enough": Susan A. Mohrman is quoted in the Marks's "Quality Circles," p. 46.

23   "a gewgaw bolted": Sapporito, "Revolt," p. 58.

24   "is not a program": Thomas McKenna is quoted by Y. K. Shetty and Vernon M. Buehler (eds.) in Productivity and Quality Through People (Westport, Ct.: Greenwood Press 1985), pp. 108–109.

24   Eaton's experience with participative techniques is described by Saporito in "Revolt," p. 64.

24   "is not the absence": Rosabeth Moss Kanter, *Change Masters* (New York: Simon and Schuster 1983), p. 248.

24   "Things that used to work": Larry Wilson is quoted by Anne Hillerman in "Larry Wilson and the Corporate Trapeze," *Southwest Airlines Spirit*, December 1986, p.90.

24   "Vehicles for greater participation": Kanter, *Change Masters*, p.241.

Chapter 3

30   Total Market Approach: "Total Market Approach," *McDonald's Operator Digest*, June 1982, pp. 1–3.

Chapter 6

86   "hoopla" is described by Terrence E. Deal and Allan A. Kennedy in *Corporate Cultures: The Rites and Rituals of Corporate Life*, (Reading, Mass.: Addison-Wesley 1982), pp. 11–13.

87   The North American Tool and Die Freezer Award is described in the videotape, *In Search of Excellence*, Boston: Nathan/Tyler Productions 1985.

Chapter 7

94   According to a survey: "Training in the Fortune 500," *Training*, July 1986, p. 61.

94   "though it seems": Daniel H. Gray, "Uses and Misuses of Strategic Planning," *Harvard Business Review*, January-February 1986, p. 89.

94   "Let's face it,": Hayes, "Awry."

95   "Companies trapped in half": Gray, "Uses and Misuses" pp. 94–95.

96   "It is now widely accepted": Ibid., p. 91.

96   "good action detailing": Ibid., p. 94.

96   "those below know": Ibid.

96   " . . . Too often,": Rae Barrett, "The SEPROD Group of Companies" A case study of the LENS Process applied to the development of a Corporate Management Style and Strategic Planning Process." Kingston, Jamaica, n.p. 1988, p. 12.

97   "Approximately seven out of ten": Gray, "Uses and Misuses," p. 94.

97   "the cure for": Ibid.

98   *In every instance :* Fred Polak is quoted by Peter Russell in *The Global Brain*, (Los Angeles: J. P. Tarcher, Inc. 1983).

98   *One of the hallmarks:* Hillerman, "Larry Wilson," p. 91.

98   *An effective organization:* John Parr is quoted by Cynthia Reedy Johnson in "An Outline for Team Building, *Training*, January 1986, p. 49.

98   *The leader is not:* Peter Senge is quoted by Walter Kiechel III in "Visionary Leadership and Beyond," *Fortune*, July 21, 1986, p. 128.

103 *The cure for:* Gray, "Uses and Misuses," p. 94.

104 *Eighty-seven per cent:* Ibid., p. 90.

110 *Our employees not only:* the quotes at the end of Chapter 7 are from letters from *ToP* clients and from participants comments during evaluation sessions of *ToP* Strategic Planning Sessions.

Chapter 8

111 *More and more companies:* The Executive Searcher from Korn Ferry is quoted by Tony Chemasi in "Power and Influence," *Success!* July–August 1986, p. 61.

111 *Managers control.:* John H. Zenger, "Leadership: Management's Better Half," *Training*, December 1985, p. 53.

114 Studies show that: C. Johnson, D.W., and Johnson, R. *Learning Together and Alone: Cooperation, Competition and Individualization.* (Englewood Cliffs, NJ: Prentice Hall, 1987).

114 The story of the Taj Group of Hotels is taken in large part from "Leadership Development," in *Image: An Action Research Journal on Organizational Transformation,* Bombay, Institute of Cultural Affairs: India, Corporate Services Division) April 1987, pp. 2–5.

115 Craig R. Hickman and Michael A. Silva. *Creating Excellence.* New York: N.A.L., 1986.

115 Myers-Briggs Type Indicator, Palo Alto, California: Consulting Psychologists Press, Inc.

115 *A Whack on the Side of the Head: How to Unlock Your Mind for Motivation* by Roger von Oech, (New York: Warner Books) 1983.

115 *The Possible Human: A Course in Extending Your Physical, Mental and Creative Abilities* by Jean Houston, (Los Angeles: J.P. Tarcher) 1982.

116 *Everything You Ever Wanted to Know About Supervision,* (Des Moines, Iowa: American Media Inc.) n.d.

117 Abraham Maslow's hierarchy of needs is described in *Motivation and Personality* by Abraham Maslow, (New York: Harper & Brothers) 1954 (second edition, 1970).

117 Herzberg's motivational theory is found in "One More Time: How do you motivate employees?" by Frederick Herzberg, *Harvard Business Review*, January-February 1968, pp. 26–35.

117 John Kenneth Galbraith, *The Anatomy of Power,* Boston: Houghton Mifflin, 1983.

117 *Leadership and the One Minute Manager,* (Escondito, California: Blanchard Training & Development) 1987.

117 Roger Harrison. "Strategies for a New Age," *Human Resource Management*, Fall 1983. Copyright 1983 by John Wiley & Sons.

117 *Twelve O'Clock High*, Fox, 1949.

117 *The Global Brain,* (Shawnee Mission, Kansas: RMI Video Productions) 1984.

Chapter 9

119 *Mission supplies the form:* David K. Hurst, "Why Strategic Management is Bankrupt," *Organizational Dynamics* (New York: American Management Association) Spring 1986, p. 17.

119 *Our endeavor is:* **Harrison, "Strategies for a New Age," p. 224.**

119 One critic of "strategic management": Hurst, "Bankrupt," pp. 8–14.

119 " a search for meaning." Harrison, Strategies for a New Age," p. 224.

121 *. . . Organization purpose is:* Ibid., p. 223.

121 *Like Janus, the Roman:* Hurst, "Bankrupt." p. 19.

127 *Every excellent company:* Peters and Waterman, "Excellence." p. 280.

130 *Everyone operates out of images:* Imaginal Education Curriculum (Chicago: Institute of Cultural Affairs)

130 Kenneth Boulding, *The Image* (Ann Arbor: The University of Michigan Press Ann Arbor Paperback 1956), Chapter 1.

136 ". . . Leadership is really": Hurst, "Bankrupt," p. 25.

Chapter 10

141 "Public Agenda Forum": Warren Bennis and Burt Nanus, *Leaders: The Strategies for Taking Charge.* Perrenial Library edition (New York: Harper & Row 1985), pp. 7–8.

142 "People want to make": Naisbitt and Aburdene, "Reinventing," p. 255.

142   "One of the best-kept": Ibid., p. 265.

142   Karen Carpenter shared the story of the Minnesota Energy Agency in an interview with ICA staff in Minneapolis in October, 1987.

143   "Ownership is a psychological": Lawrence M. Miller, *American Spirit: Views of a New Corporate Culture*, (New York: Morrow) 1984, p. 75.

143   "What are the keys": Ibid., p. 82.

144   "the employee on all levels": Peter Drucker, *Managing in Turbulent Times*, (New York: Harper & Row) 1980, pp. 192–193.

144   "I think the most": Jack Sheehan describes his encounters with **ToP** in the video, *Chicago: A Passion for Participation*, (Chicago: Institute of Cultural Affairs) 1987.

144   "the need to involve": Rosabeth Moss Kanter and Barry A. Stein, "Much Ado About Management," *The Rotarian*, November 1986, p. 17.

145   "The successful manager": Miller, *American Spirit*. p. 46.

145   "good leadership at": Michael Maccoby, *The Leader: A New Face for American Management,* (New York: Simon & Schuster) 1981, p.21.

145   "We continually emphasize": Ray Stata is quoted by Charles Kiefer and Peter M. Senge in "Metanoic Organizations in the Transition to a Sustainable Society," a   paper presented at the Woodlands Conference, July 1982, p. 17.

146   "people who get": Miller, American Spirit, p.55.

Chapter 11

147   "When the diverse elements": Karen Wilhelm Buckley and Joan Steffy, "The Invisible Side of Leadership," from *Transforming Leadership: From Vision to Results*, by John Adams (ed.), (Alexandria, VA: Miles River Press) 1986, p. 238.

147   "the realization within": Kiefer and Senge, "Metanoic Organizations," p. 29.

148   "In the two years": George Hazler's comments as well as the story of Mount Carmel Mercy Hospital are taken from the untitled videotape depicting Mt. Carmel's success, referred to in Chapter 1 notes.

148   "The new corporate leader": Miller, *American Spirit*, p. 46.

148   The story of Copper Mountain Ski Resort was shared with us in November, 1987, by Marty Seldman, the consultant who facilitated their planning session.

150   "cowboy management,": Rosabeth Moss Kanter, "Management at the O.K. Corral," *Savvy*, October 1986, p. 36.

150   "Some curtail it": Zenger, "Better Half," p. 46.

150   "Although my staff": William H. Peace, "I Thought I Knew What Good ManageMent Was," *Harvard Business Review,* March-April 1986, p. 65.

151   The story of The Pas Lumber Company is taken largely from a report prepared by the president, Don Gould in July, 1987.

151   "typically involve themselves": Kiefer and Senge, "Metanoic Organizations. p. 19.

152   "You put a group": James Capraro's comments are from the video, *Chicago: A Passion for Excellence*.

152   "the task force": Peters and Waterman, *Excellence*, p. 132.

152   Russ Goodman related the story of the Department of Human Services of the State of Minnesota in an interview with ICA staff in Minneapolis in November, 1987.

Chapter 12

155   "In the new information-rich": Naisbitt and Aburdene, *Reinventing*, p. 136.

155   "Management is heading toward": Perry Pascarella. *The New Achievers: Creating a Modern Work Ethic*, (New York: Free Press) 1984.

155   "We're not really sure": Peters and Waterman, *Excellence*, p. 218.

156   "The most common roadblock": Kanter, *The Change Masters*, p. 160.

156   "innovating companies seem": Ibid., p. 167.

156   "The trouble with much": Theodore Levitt. "Ideas are Useless Unless Used," *Inc.*, February 1981, p. 96.

157   "innovation does not just": Cass Bettinger. "If Response to Change is So Important, Why Is No One In Charge?" *American Banker*, April 25, 1986.

157 "*Fortune* magazine's eight": Naisbitt and Aburdene, *Reinventing* p. 32.

158 "A major consequence" Russell L. Ackoff, *Creating the Corporate Future: Plan or be Planned For*, (New York: John Wiley & Sons) 1981, pp. 71–73.

158 a study by consultant Richard G. Allen: Robert Heller, *The Supermanagers*, (New York: E.P. Dutton) 1985, pp. 231–232.

158 "87% reported feelings": Gray, "Uses and Misuses," p. 90.

159 "Separate the responsibility": Heller, *The Supermanagers*, p. 229.

160 "The ICA has been uniformly successful:" Art Vazquez's comments are taken from the video, *Chicago: A Passion for Participation.*

160 "For the first time": Mayor Harold Washington's comments are from the video, *Chicago: A Passion for Participation.*

Bibliography

Books

Ackoff, Russell L. *Creating the Corporate Future: Plan or be Planned For*. New York: John Wiley & Sons, 1981.

Adams, John, ed. *Transforming Leadership: From Vision to Results*. Alexandria, VA: Miles River Press, 1986.

Anthony, William P. *Participative Management*. Reading, Mass.: Addison-Wesley, 1978.

Bennis, Warren and Nanus, Burt. *Leaders: The Strategies for Taking Charge*. New York: Harper & Row (Perrenial Library edition), 1985.

Boulding, Kenneth. *The Image*. Ann Arbor: The University of Michigan Press (Ann Arbor Paperback), 1956.

Burns, James MacGregor. *Leadership*. New York: Harper & Row, 1978.

Deal, Terrence E. and Kennedy, Allan A. *Corporate Cultures: The Rites and Rituals of Corporate Life*. Reading, Mass.: Addison-Wesley, 1982.

Drucker, Peter. *Managing in Turbulent Times*. New York: Harper & Row, 1980.

Galbraith, John Kenneth. *Anatomy of Power*. Boston: Houghton Mifflin, 1983.

Heller, Robert. *The Supermanagers*. New York: E.P. Dutton, 1985.

Hickman, Craig R. and Silva, Michael A. *Creating Excellence*. New York: N.A.L., 1986.

Houston, Jean. *The Possible Human: A Course in Extending Your Physical, Mental and Creative Abilities*. Los Angeles: J.P. Tarcher, 1982.

Johnson, Spencer and Wilson, Larry. *The One Minute Salesperson: the Quickest Way to More Sales with Less Stress*. New York: William Morrow, 1984.

Kanter, Rosabeth Moss. *Change Masters*. New York: Simon and Schuster, 1983.

Maccoby, Michael. *The Leader: A New Face for American Management*. New York: Simon & Schuster, 1981.

Maslow, Abraham. *Motivation and Personality* New York: Harper & Brothers, 1954 (second edition, 1970).

McKenna, Regis. *The Regis Touch*. Reading, Mass.: Addison-Wesley, 1985.

Miller, Lawrence M. *American Spirit: Views of a New Corporate Culture*. New York: Morrow, 1984.

Oech, Roger von. *A Whack on the Side of the Head: How to Unlock Your Mind for Motivation*. New York: Warner Books, 1983.

Pascarella, Perry. *The New Achievers: Creating a Modern Work Ethic*. New York: Free Press, 1984.

Russell, Peter. *The Global Brain*. Los Angeles: J. P. Tarcher, 1983.

Sayles, Leonard R. *Leadership: What Effective Managers Do . . . and How They Do It*. New York: McGraw Hill, 1979.

Shetty, Y. K. and Buehler, Vernon M. (eds.). *Productivity and Quality Through People*. Westport, Ct.: Greenwood Press, 1985.

Solman, Paul and Friedman, Thomas. *Life and Death on the Corporate Battlefield*. New York: Simon & Schuster, 1982.

Whyte, William H. *The Organization Man*. New York: Simon & Schuster, 1956.

Articles

Bettinger, Cass. "If Response to Change is So Important, Why Is No One In Charge?" *American Banker*, April 25, 1986.

Buckley, Karen Wilhelm and Steffy, Joan. "The Invisible Side of Leadership." In *Transforming Leadership: From Vision to Results*, pp. 233–243. Edited by John Adams. Alexandria, VA: Miles River Press, 1986.

Chemasi, Tony. "Power and Influence." *Success*! July–August 1986, p. 61.

Crockett, William J. "The Emerging World of the Manger." (mimeographed) n.p., n.d.

Forrester, Jay. "A New Corporate Design." *Industrial Management Review*. Cambridge, Mass. M.I.T.'s Sloan School of Management, Fall 1965. vol.7, No. 1.

Gray, Daniel H. "Uses and Misuses of Strategic Planning." *Harvard Business Review*, January-February, 1986, pp. 89–97.

Harrison, Roger. "Strategies for a New Age." *Human Resource Management*, Fall 1983, Copyright 1983 by John Wiley & Sons.

Hayes, Robert H. "Why Strategic Planning Goes Awry." *New York Times*, April 20, 1986, p. 2F.

Herzberg, Frederick. "One More Time: How do you motivate employees?" *Harvard Business Review*, January-February, 1968, pp. 26–35.

Hillerman, Anne. "Larry Wilson and the Corporate Trapeze," by Anne Hillerman. *Southwest Airlines Spirit*, December, 1986, p. 40.

Hurst, David K. "Why Strategic Management is Bankrupt." *Organizational Dynamics*, New York: American Management Association, Spring 1986, pp. 5–27.

Johnson, Cynthia Reedy. "An Outline for Team Building." *Training*, January 1986, pp. 48–52.

Kanter, Rosabeth Moss. "Management at the O.K. Corral." *Savvy*, October 1986, p. 36.

Kanter, Rosabeth Moss and Stein, Barry A. "Much Ado About Management." *The Rotarian*, November 1986, pp. 14–17.

Kiechel, Walter III. "Visionary Leadership and Beyond." *Fortune*, July 21, 1986, pp. 27–28.

Kiefer, Charles and Senge, Peter M. "Metanoic Organizations in the Transition to a Sustainable Society," Woodlands Conference, July 1982.

"Leadership Development." *Image: An Action Research Journal on Organizational Transformation*, Bombay: ICA: India, Corporate Services Division, April 1987, pp. 2–5.

Levitt, Theodore. "Ideas are Useless Unless Used," *Inc.*, February 1981.

Marks, Mitchell Lee. "The Question of Quality Circles." *Psychology Today*. March 1986, p. 36.

Peace, William H. "I Thought I Knew What Good Management Was." *Harvard Business Review*, March-April 1986.

Prokesch, Steven. "Remaking the American C.E.O." *New York Times*, January 25, 1987, Section 3, p. 1.

Sapporito, Bill. "The Revolt Against Working Smarter," *Fortune* July 21, 1986, pp. 58–65

Shashkin, Marshall. "Participative Management Remains an Ethical Imperative." *Organizational Dynamics*, (AMA Periodicals Review), Spring 1982, pp. 62-75.

Shashkin, Marshall. "A Manager's Guide to Participative Management" (American Management Association Briefing). New York: AMA Membership Publications Division, 1982.

"Total Market Approach." *McDonald's Operator Digest*, June 1982, pp. 1–3.

"Training in the Fortune 500." *Training*, July 1986, p. 61.

Yankelovich, Daniel and Immerwahr, John. "Putting the Work Ethic to Work: a Public Agenda Report on Restoring America's Competitive Vitality." New York: Public Agenda Foundation, 1983.

Zenger, John H. "Leadership: Management's Better Half." *Training*, December 1985, pp. 44–53.

Videos and Films

Everything You Ever Wanted to Know About Supervision. Des Moines, Iowa: American Media Inc., n.d.

In Search of Excellence, Boston: Nathan/Tyler Productions, 1985.

Leadership and the One Minute Manager. Escondito, California: Blanchard Training & Development, Inc., 1987.

The Global Brain. Shawnee Mission, Kansas: RMI Video Productions, Inc. 1984.

A Passion for Participation. Chicago: Institute of Cultural Affairs, 1987.

Twelve O'Clock High. Fox, 1949.

Untitled video. Detroit: Audio Visual Services, Mt. Carmel Mercy Hospital, 1985.

INDEX

178

ABOUT THE ICA

The Institute of Cultural Affairs is a private, non-profit organization concerned with the human factor in world development. Formerly a research division of the Ecumenical Institute, the ICA was separately incorporated in 1972 to promote the design and application of methods for human development in communities and organizations. The ICA carries out its mission through a variety of programs and services.

The ICA offers consultancy services in a variety of fields, applying the *Technology of Participation (ToP)* for strategic planning, leadership development and organizational transformation.

Education and training programs offered by the ICA focus on participatory planning and problem solving techniques, consensus processes, team building, curriculum design and educational methods.

The ICA's research programs are action-oriented and focused on the integration of methods of human consciousness and organizational transformation. Specific areas of research include the dynamics of social change, ethical frameworks, personal roles, learning patterns, corporate philosophy and values and profound life understandings.

Twenty-eight nationally chartered and registered ICA's are linked through the Institute of Cultural Affairs International (ICAI), comprising a network of 54 centers in North and South America, Africa, Europe, India, Asia and the Pacific. The ICAI is headquartered in Brussels. Worldwide, there are approximately 500 full-time ICA staff from a variety of backgrounds. They are complemented by an equal number of people working in part-time capacities to support and facilitate ICA programs.

The strength of the ICA lies in its ability to bring together experience in human resource development from a variety of situations, ranging from village projects to international organizations. It works with people from the private, public, voluntary and local sectors of society. The central concern of its diverse programs is to maximize the participation of people in the process of taking responsibility for their own lives and for society as a whole.

For further information about *ToP* facilitation, training, or other programs of the Institute of Cultural Affairs, contact the nearest ICA office.

AFRICA

Ivory Coast
Institute des Affaires Culturelles
B.P. 119
Brobo
Cote d'Ivoire

Kenya
Institute of Cultural Affairs
P.O. Box 21679
Nairobi
Kenya
Tel: (254 2) 724314 or 7293375

Nigeria
Nigerian Integrated Rural Accelerated
Development Organization (NIRADO)
GPO Box 2524
Lagos
Nigeria
Tel: daytime messages
Mr. A. M. Sharta (234 1) 631 990 or
Mr. F. N. Akpe (234 1) 610 430
Fax: (234 1) 617 565, ATTN: F. N. Akpe

Zambia
Institute of Cultural Affairs
P.O. Box 31454
10101 Lusaka
Zambia
Tel: (260 1) 252 825 / 226 348

ASIA

Australia
The Institute of Cultural Affairs
GPO Box 1792
Sydney, NSW 2001
Australia
Tel: (61 2) 560–9876 / 896–3839
Fax: (61 2) 564–2760 / 631–3239

Hong Kong
Institute of Cultural Affairs
Woodside, Mount Parker Road
Quarry Bay
Hong Kong
Tel: (852 5) 626 181
Fax: (852 5) 260 0747

India
Institute of Cultural Affairs: India
13 Sankli Street, 2nd Floor
Byculla, Bombay 400 008
India
Tel: (91 22) 308 7751
Fax: (91 22) 942 222 ATTN: ICA

Institute of Cultural Affairs: India
25 Nav Jivan Vihar
New Delhi, 110 017
India
Tel: (91 11) 652 871
Fax: (91 11) 688 3369

Institute of Cultural Affairs: India
Plot 7, Road 10, Sector 1
New Panvel 410 217
India
Tel: (91 22) 745–1542
Fax: (91 22) 745–1083 ATTN: ICA

Institute of Cultural Affairs: India
D-2 Vidhyamrut Coop. Housing Society
9 Shankarseth Road
Pune 411 037
India
Tel: (91–21) 265–2906

Japan
Institute of Cultural Affairs
Seijo 2–38–4–102
Setagaya-ku
Tokyo 157, Japan
Tel: (81 3) 3416–7558
Fax: (81 3) 3416–0499

Malaysia
LENS International Malaysia Sdn. Bhd.
P.O. Box 10564
50718, Kuala Lumpur
Malaysia
Tel: (603) 757–5604
Fax: (603) 756–4420

Republic of China
Institute of Cultural Affairs
6th Floor, 53–1, Chung Shan North Road
Section 7
Tien Mou, Taipei 11136
Taiwan
Tel: (886–2) 871–3150
Fax: (886–2) 871–4648

Republic of Korea
ICA Korea
KPO Box 1052
Seoul
Republic of Korea
Tel: (82–2) 733–3520
Fax: (82–2) 733–3255

Republic of the Philippines
The Institute of Cultural Affairs
Philippines
603 Boni Avenue, Mandaluyong
1501 Metro Manila
Republic of the Philippines
Tel: (63) 278–0071–4, local 6
Fax: (63) 278–0074

EUROPE

Belgium
Institut des Affaires Culturelles
rue Amedee Lynen 8
B-1030 Brussels,
Belgium
Tel: (32–2) 219–0087
Fax: (32–2) 219–0406

Germany
Institute of Cultural Affairs e.V.
Darmstaedter Landstrasse 109
6000 Frankfurt / Main 70
Germany
Tel: (49 69) 618753

Portugal
Instituto de Assuntos Culturais
Apartado 35
5101 Lamego Codex
Portugal

Rue Central 28, Mezio
3600 Castro Daire
Portugal
Tel: (351 54) 68246
Fax: (351 54) 68246 or 62045
ATTN: ICA

Spain
Instituto de Asuntos Culturales
Santelmo, 83
28016 Madrid
Spain
Tel: (34 1) 250 0088

United Kingdom
Institute of Cultural Affairs
P.O. Box 505
London N19 3YX
United Kingdom

LATIN AMERICA

Brazil
Instituto de Assuntos Culturais
Avenida Graca Aranha 416, sala 1116
20030 Rio de Janeiro, RJ
Brazil
Tel: (55 21) 242–4445 / 507–1360
(weekdays)
(55 21) 228–2159 / 248–6454 (evenings)
Fax: (55 21) 252–8402

Chile
c/o Eduardo Schulze Christensen
Cruz del Sur 367
Las Condes
Santiago
Chile
Tel: (56–2) 228–7602

Guatemala
Instituto de Asuntos Culturales de
Guatemala
13 Calle 15–68, Zona 1 001001
Cuidad Guatemala
Guatemala, C.A.
Tel: (502 2) 29792
Fax: (502 2) 84790—Access

Mexico
Instituto de Asuntos Culturales
Unidad Agua Caliente 11
Calle Agua Caliente 129
Edif. 8, Depto. 204
Colonia Pantitlan
08100 Mexico, D.F.
Mexico
Fax: (52 322) 80296

Peru
Instituto de Asuntos Culturales
Apartado 11–0630
Lima, 11
Peru
Tel: (51 14) 610813
Fax: (51 14) 610813

Venezuela
ICA Venezuela
Apartado 5842
Caracas 1010 A
Venezuela
Tel (58 2) 261–5276 / 5819
Fax: (58 2) 951–3449 c/o John Lawton

MIDDLE EAST

Egypt
The Institute of Cultural Affairs:
Middle East and North Africa
1079 Corniche El Nil Garden City
Cairo
Arab Republic of Egypt
Tel: (20 2) 352–2584 (Cairo)
(20 82) 352–4133 (Bayad el Arab)
Fax: (20 2) 352 2584 (Cairo)
(20 82) 224 269 (Bayad El Arab)

NORTH AMERICA

Canada

ICA Canada
577 Kingston Road Suite #1
Toronto, Ontario M4E 1R3
Canada
Tel: (1 416) 691–2316
Fax: (1 416) 619–2491

United States of America

Institute of Cultural Affairs
4750 North Sheridan Road
Chicago, Illinois 60640
U.S.A.
Tel: (1 312) 769–6363
Fax: (1 312) 769–1141

Institute of Cultural Affairs
629 E. 5th Street
New York, New York 10029–6824
U.S.A.
Tel: (1 212) 673–5984
Fax: (1 212) 505–1548

ICA West
4220 N. 25th Street
Phoenix, Arizona 85016
U.S.A.
Tel: (1–602) 955–4811
Fax: (1 602) 954–0506

ABOUT THE AUTHOR

Laura Spencer ''grew up'' with the *Technology of Participation* since the age of thirteen when her family joined the staff of the ICA. She was first exposed to the methods in their early form as she participated in neighborhood youth organizations sponsored by the ICA in its first community renewal project on Chicago's west side.

While a student at the University of Illinois, Ms. Spencer used *ToP* methods as study tools. She earned credit for her work with the ICA in developing several applications of *ToP*. These included the *ToP Strategic Planning Process,* the Fifth City Social Model and research into the dynamics of social change, which led to the ICA's application of *ToP* methods in thousands of communities around the world. Ms. Spencer received a B.A. with honors in History and Sociology and teaching certification in 1973.

Like most ICA staff, Ms. Spencer's experience in applying *ToP* methods ranges from socio-economic planning in the villages of developing nations to strategic planning for multi-national corporations. A gifted communicator, she has contributed to many of the ICA's publications and served as communications coordinator for the International Exposition of Rural Development.

Ms. Spencer's skills in communication and application of *ToP* methods were combined to bring forth from the ICA the book you now hold in your hands.